THE Honey POT

Sister Femi

THE *Honey* POT

Sister Femi

The Honey Pot

copyright © Sister Femi 2020

All rights reserved

Enquiries should be addressed to:
olufemioluboyede@gmail.com
Instagram: @Sister.Femi

ISBN 978 978 977 644 3

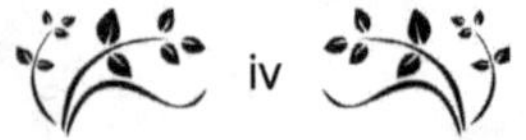

DEDICATION

This book is dedicated to my children, Otunloluwa and Folusade, and every Nigerian youth. You are not lazy! Rise up in righteousness, occupy you place and fulfil your destinies!

ACKNOWLEDGEMENT

First and foremost, praises and thanks to God, the Almighty, for choosing me to write this book. Lord I am grateful for your revelation and presence now and always. It is such a great joy to be loved by You.

I would like to express my deep and sincere gratitude to my biological and spiritual children for all their trust in sharing with me their challenges, confusion, and desire for understanding God's heart regarding relationship, sex, and marriage. Your inquisitive hearts for the truth really helped me to be diligent in seeking God's face for revelation concerning this book.

My profound gratitude also goes to my dear friend, Adedoyin Adebayo. I appreciate your support and prayers throughout the writing of this book. Thank you for making sure I meet the deadline. May the Lord reward you abundantly.

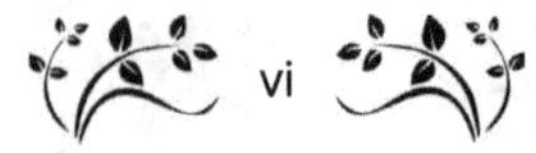

My thanks go to my family and all the people who have supported me to complete this work directly or indirectly. I pray that you will all fulfill God's purpose for your lives in Jesus name.

INTRODUCTION

Dear Reader,

Before you start reading this book, let me tell you this - Do not be in a rush to get to the end; be patient while you read and take your time to understand what is written on every page, because this book is intended to expose a lot of hidden secrets about sex and marriage.

May I also say that, as you read on, no matter which category you fall into regarding the main subject matter or any sub-topic in this book, make sure you don't feel discouraged or condemned in any way, as that is not the purpose of this book. I believe strongly what the word of God says in *Romans 8:1 that "There is therefore now no condemnation to those who are in Christ Jesus, who do not walk according to the flesh but according to the Spirit."* The Word and revelations from God are never to condemn us; though it may condemn what we are doing, when it is not according to the will of God. The

same Word and revelation are profitable to us for doctrine, for reproof, for correction and instruction in righteousness.

Through the help of the Holy Spirit, we will try as much as possible to expose the extent of damage that has been done because of generic misunderstanding of the purpose and power of marriage and sexual intercourse, and for us to be able to know where to ask for repair works to begin from, so that we can eventually appreciate the result. Just like when your car is faulty , you will take it to your auto engineer, who will diagnose the problem and advise on the type of repair work that needs to be carried out, and thereafter goes ahead to repair the damage. By the time the repair is complete, and your car starts moving again, you will be able to appreciate the work that has been done on your car.

Remember, this book is not intended to condemn. Make sure you read to the end because for every issue highlighted, God (in His infinite mercy) already has a solution proffered. He is not

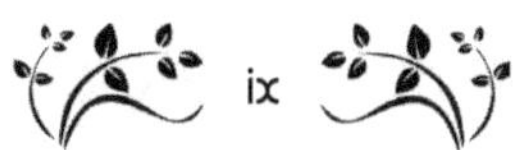

bringing this book your way to make you feel small, condemned or guilty, but rather to let you know how much He loves you, and that no matter the damage that might have been done, He can fix it for you as He does not want you to be cheated out of any of your inheritance in Him.

Marriage and sexual intercourse have been put in place by God from the beginning of the world for our benefit and enjoyment; but the enemy (the devil) continues to prey on our ignorance and had turned them into a tool of destruction and setback against us. But by the grace of God, not anymore! So, let us start this journey of discoveries together.

Table of Contents

CHAPTER 1

Let us start from the popular understanding of marriage. I believe marriage is one of the topics that most of us wish we have more insight into before we plunged in. One common saying is true though - Marriage is the only institution where you receive your certification at the point of entry instead of at the end or should I say there is no certificate designed for the end because there should not be an end anyway (it is designed to be "till death do us part"). Is it an error that the marriage institution is designed that way? Definitely not! God is perfect and in Him there is no mistake at all.

"He has made everything beautiful in his time. Also, He has put eternity in their hearts, except that

no one can find out the work that God does from beginning to end. (Ecclesiastes 3:11).

There are two things I want us to pay attention to in this bible verse.

➢ The first one is that God has made everything beautiful in its time, therefore, His design for marriage is perfect and beautiful for the people he has created in His image. Whether we are enjoying our marriage and its attendant benefits or not is now dependent on our understanding and acceptance of the original form and design of the marriage institution.

➢ The second is that God has placed eternity in our hearts — a sense of divine purpose. It will be wrong for us to think that ministerial call or some other work relating to serving humanity is all there is to divine purpose. Everything God has created and set in place is for a particular divine purpose, even marriage. Going into marriage for just any other reason like:

- *Seeking to be loved*

- *Companionship.*

- *To signify a life-long commitment.*

- *To provide security for children.*

- *To make a public commitment to each other.*

- *For legal status and financial security.*

- *For religious beliefs.*

- *For social status, and such others*

Without adequate consideration for the divine purpose intended in its foundation, will be a very costly mistake, and the result of this will be that the available blessings and benefits of the marriage institution would not be fully accessed; and the people in such marriage would often wonder why on earth they got married.

There has always been a longing in me to know more about sex and marriage as intended by God.

This longing was birthed by my observation that many good people are experiencing great difficulties in their marriages and sex life. Often times, the two people in a marriage would be fantastic whenever they operate or interact with the external world individually, but when they get together at home, different personalities entirely are revealed. I began to wonder, what exactly is wrong? I have flipped through pages of the Bible, armed with the understanding I have gathered from marriage seminars, sermons, books amongst others; but I only saw what I have heard or read before. At a certain point, I got tired of reading books on marriage and sex. Not because they are not beautifully written. No, far from that. In fact, I stand in no position under heaven to criticize any writing, big or small. You know why? I dislike writing with passion. So, when I see books and write-ups, I see it as a great work done by great and patient people. My reason for not being excited about books relating to sex or marriage is simply because the few I have come across did not answer most of my questions. In my opinion, a lot of them seem tailored after personal

experiences and observations. Same goes for most teachings on marriage. I believe marriage and sex are quite significant and fundamental to human existence, that trying to understand or explain it from personal experiences or observations would only lead to more confusion, instead of clarity. There is no way two people will react to an issue the same way, even if they are identical twins. In fact, it is said that if there is a crime that police need to get eyewitness reports for, they do not expect any two reports to be the same, because perspective and opinion from one witness to another will surely be different. Obtaining very similar reports from different eyewitnesses would certainly raise suspicions. So, for us to grasp a good understanding of marriage and sex, books and teaching based on an author's personal experiences and observations will only help, when the fundamental design is understood from God's point of view.

A few weeks after a protest in my home country, Nigeria, against a statement made by the President regarding the nation's youth in 2018, God began to

open my eyes to scriptures pertaining to mysteries surrounding marriage and sexual intercourse. This started after I have given up on trying to understand or look for answer regarding these subjects. That God would decide in His perfect wisdom to choose someone like me to write this book is one of the greatest humors of creation; even Gideon's story in the bible, would appear far less humorous. Anyway, like I mentioned earlier, God does not make mistakes, the bible tells us:

"But God has chosen the foolish things of the world to put to shame the wise, and God has chosen the weak things of the world to put to shame the things which are mighty" *(1 Corinthians 1:27).*

I am a living example!

If the revelations and the insights you will read about in this book are truly from God; no matter where you stand in life at the time of reading this book, you should never feel condemned, but liberated, because the word of God *says "And you*

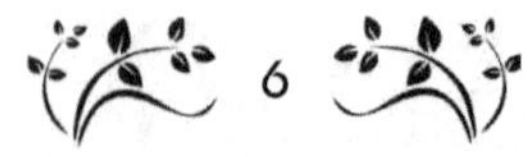

shall know the truth, and the truth shall make you free" (John 8:32). When the truth is revealed to the heart of man, it divinely inspires such peace that is beyond human explanation; and this peace in turn brings about liberation, freedom, and motion in the right direction. *And "there is therefore now no condemnation for those who are in Christ Jesus, who work not after the flesh but after the spirit" (Romans 8:1).*

I have always wondered why there are so many challenges in many marriages, often to the point of depression, physical abuse, spiritual attacks and ultimately divorce in some instances. Where exactly did we get it wrong, especially in Christendom? Not that the problem is with only Christians, I just think that since we believe in the finished work of redemption on the Cross of Calvary, we believe in God's Word and have received the Holy Spirit - our marriages should be relatively blissful, without pain, without stress and simply be heaven on earth. You will be amazed that two people that are not even born-again, if they somehow manage to get the marriage

fundamentals right, they would have inadvertently excused themselves from almost eighty percent (80%) of marital challenges. Their major challenge might only then be the lack of guidance for their divine purpose on earth; that is, though they have a great start, they would have a faulty finish.

MAN-MADE APPROACH

I know many of us have been taught in marriage seminars and churches about the search for marital partners, courting and marriage. We have been advised to pay attention to and observe a lot of things about the person we are planning to marry, his or her family history too; and that by observations, we would be able to know if the person matches our expectation of a suitable future partner. Our parents might even go a step further by carrying out further family background checks. However, how have all these observations and checks really helped marriages? Do not get me wrong. I am not saying taking those steps are not good, but they should not be the main focus. There are lots of marriages that their due diligence during courtship were top-notch, yet, unexpected troubles seem to start almost immediately after the wedding ceremonies. I am not saying there are no good marriages; what I am saying is that the percentage is so negligible and incomparable or not close to God's desire for us. Marital pain and struggle are not the will of God for us, but they have arisen as we have embraced man-made doctrines on marriage and have neglected God's original ordained plan. No matter what modern culture implies, the laid down path and plan of God for marriage has not changed and it will never change. A man needs to totally depend on God when deciding on a suitable marital partner, just like Adam did without any interference with God's choice of a partner for him. It was not a temporary plan from God that must be put away when the real plan becomes available. This plan of total dependence on God for a partner was established from the beginning of man, before sin came in; it is the perfect plan ordained for man before the world began.

"And the Lord God caused a deep sleep to fall on Adam, and he slept; and He took one of his ribs and closed up the flesh in its place. Then the rib which the Lord God had taken from man He made into a woman, and He brought her to the man" (Genesis 2: 20-21).

If after Adam, who was in the perfect image of God, without corruption, needed to be put to deep sleep, to show him that, though he has been given charge over everything on the surface of the earth, the only contribution that will be needed from him to receive a suitable partner is to take a position of rest in God, then we should know that if we want a suitable partner, we too need to take that position of rest in God. To rest in God is to believe completely in what He says in His Word regarding everything. It is having faith in Him. Living by faith is not a struggle but rest. When you hope for marriage according to God's design, you must exercise your faith regarding that hope.

"Now faith is the substance of things hoped for, the evidence of things not seen." Hebrews 11:1

This simply means if you need healing, go into the word of God and find out what He says about healing and believe it. That scripture is the substance of the thing (healing) that you hope for, the evidence of things (healing) not seen. That scripture is your faith! Your faith is found in His Word.

"So then faith *comes* by hearing, and hearing by the word of God." Romans 10:17.

Faith in God must be applied to every aspect of our lives including our choice of marriage partners. When you ask Him, you receive what you ask for. See how Jesus made it clear how God does not want to be misunderstood about His willingness and ability to give good things to His children in this passage:

"Ask, and it will be given to you; seek, and you will find; knock, and it will be opened to you. For everyone who asks receives, and he who seeks finds, and to him who knocks it will be opened. Or what man is there among you who, if his son asks for bread, will give him a stone? Or if he asks for a fish, will he give him a serpent? If you then, being evil, know how

to give good gifts to your children, how much more will your Father who is in heaven give good things to those who ask Him! Therefore, whatever you want men to do to you, do also to them, for this is the Law and the Prophets." Mathew 7:7-12

When Jesus finished his comparison between human parents (with evil nature) and God as a heavenly Father, see what he concluded with in verse 12: *whatever you want men to do to you, do also to them.* Wow! You know, this is just like when you are not happy that people are misunderstanding who you really are in the presence of obvious facts. Jesus was telling them plainly that you being evil do good things for your children and you will not want anyone to think otherwise of you, therefore don't think of my your heavenly Father the way you will not want people to think of you. It did not sound like a gentle conversation at all, but Jesus could not just stand people having wrong opinion about the heavenly Father. I love that! Taking a position of rest in God by believing in Him to choose the right marital partner for you is the starting point, the real deal, the solid foundation.

Some people are of the opinion that once a prospective partner is born-again, it is okay to marry such a person. However, I am clarifying emphatically, that if you really desire to fulfil the purpose of God for your life, you cannot afford to marry anyone just because he or she is born-again. Of course, you would not be committing any sin by marrying a born-again Christian, but you may end up living a struggle-filled and frustrated life if your purpose is quite different from your chosen partner's. There will be a *"joining together"*; but there will not be *"becoming one flesh"*. The marriage of two people that have the same purpose and vision is not necessarily challenge-free, because devil will always attack all good things; now imagine a marriage of two people with differing visions and purposes. This is akin to a civil war between two different purposes; each trying to find expression; and a house that is divided against itself cannot stand. Even where the wife sacrificially submits to the purpose of her husband, they still cannot have 100% yield of fulfilment because no single person in a marriage can shoulder the full 100% of the purpose's fulfilment. Your partner has a certain percentage that he or she must bring to the table; once you make a wrong marital partner choice, your marriage is short of the required complementing percentage, you may even end up losing part of the percentage you already possess while trying to survive and stay sane in a frustrated marriage. Remember that Eve was not created freshly from the dust of the ground; she was made from a rib that was taken from Adam. Amazing, right? From just a rib from Adam! Let us ponder on this for a bit - Adam is a whole man, less a rib; and Eve is that missing rib for him. That means Adam plus Eve equals one whole man or one whole flesh because the bible says:

"Therefore, a man shall leave his father and mother and be joined to his wife, and they shall become one flesh" (Genesis 2:24).

I believe that every man has his own wife prepared for him from his rib by God. It is amazing that some members of the body of Christ often try to explain this concept away, while even secular wise men would always pray for men seeking marital partners that *"you will not choose another man's bone(rib)."* The Word of God remains ever true!

Regarding marriage, we cannot afford to stop at the level which states that:

"Do not be unequally yoked together with unbelievers. For what fellowship has righteousness with lawlessness? And what communion has light with darkness?" (2 Corinthians 6:14).

This is a level for babies in Christ, and not for those who have attained full age. Full-aged Christians are described like this:

"But solid food belongs to those who are of full age, that is, those who by reason of use have their senses exercised to discern both good and evil" (Hebrews 5:14)

Full-aged Christians have moved to the level of which states:

"Can two walks together unless they are agreed?" (Amos 3:3)

Paul and Barnabas in the bible had to part ways, and not over doctrinal differences. In fact, both were on fire for the Lord, but one believed that John Mark was a good company for the journey ahead, while the other disagreed. These two wonderful firebrand servants of the Lord had to go their separate ways because they could not agree on who should accompany them on the apostolic journey ahead of them. Their disagreement does not imply that either of them is not for the Lord, but I see it as both of them being zealous to walk the journey the way the spirit of the Lord has enabled their understanding according to their personal purpose. The events were recorded in the bible as examples for our guidance. Therefore, I submit that the fact that a brother or sister is born-again is not enough reason to assume that he or she is a suitable partner for you. There must be unity in plan, purpose and pursuit for a woman to be a suitable companion or a helpmeet for a man. Please, let us move from the elementary way of choosing a marriage partner to the ordained way by God, so we can fully benefit from the blessings He has prepared for us in marriage.

If being born-again alone is enough qualification for two Christians to get married, why then do we have so many divorce and separation in the body of Christ? Many couples that pretend as if all is well outside, are arch enemies behind closed doors. This shows that something is fundamentally wrong; possibly something that we are not yet paying enough attention to. Problems with marriages are hurting the family, society and body of Christ badly. It is about time we rise in righteousness and put an end to it.

Let us consider our ultimate example now, Jesus. The Bible records that Jesus loves the church so much, that He laid down His live for her and that man, in like manner, should love his wife. Jesus does not consider the physical appearance, wealth or capacity of the church, when He expresses His love for the church. His love for the church is not based on what He sees in the physical, it is based on the purpose of God for the church that matches His own purpose for coming to the world. Jesus was to lay down His life for humanity and build His Church;

the Church's role in return is to enforce Kingdom authority on earth. The Church, which is the body of Christ, is the suitable partner (bride) for Jesus (our Bridegroom). Both the Bride & Bridegroom, coming together in unity, are to establish the will and purpose of God upon the earth. The basis of Jesus' love for the church is to fulfil God's purpose. The presence of God's purpose does not however guarantee an absence of betrayal, challenges, and pain; but the only thing that kept Jesus till the end is the common purpose that exists in His relationship with the Church. In fact, it got to a certain point Jesus was willing to break the engagement because of limitations of the flesh (remember Jesus was manifested in flesh). He prayed in the Garden of Gethsemane, that he wished the wedding date could be cancelled:

"and he went a little farther, and fell on his face, and prayed, saying, O my Father, if it be possible, let this cup pass from me: nevertheless not as I will, but as thou wilt" (Mathew 26:39).

However, when he remembered the purpose,

though he was lacking the human power and will to carry on, he wisely submitted to the father for His will to be done. If Jesus' love was based on the physical appearance of the church then, there will be nothing like salvation today.

Therefore, a man is admonished to love his wife as Christ loves the church. You can only have power to love as Christ loved the church. when you allow God to choose for you. When you know His plan for you and your spouse, and you are sure you both agree on purpose and complete one another. Otherwise, the marriage becomes lifetime of struggles. Strength to *fight till the end* comes when you are sure that you have the backing of heaven on a course.

HOW DO I FIND?

As we all know, no man has the capacity to see into the future without the spirit of God. So, no man can by himself in the physical realm, identify his God-ordained wife that he is supposed to find in order to

obtain favour from God is, except he is being led by the Spirit of God. It is the Holy Spirit that knows the pre-ordained plan of God for everyone, that call people by what they are created to be, not by what they presently appear to be. It is that Spirit of God; that can tell, reveal to, or help a man to identify his God ordained wife. It is then that such man can obtain favour from God. Jesus, when asked by his disciples to teach them how to pray, said this "In this manner, therefore, pray:

> *Our Father in heaven,*
> *Hallowed be Your name.*
> *Your kingdom come.*
> *Your will be done*
> *On earth as it is in heaven." (Mathew 6:9-13)*

Christians are meant to live out, here on earth, the purpose that was mapped out for their lives in heaven; that is, our daily lives including our marriages have already been fashioned out in heaven. That is why Jesus taught us to pray that God's kingdom should come. His Will for our lives is to be done here on earth as it has already been settled in heaven.

We must therefore stay connected to heaven, if we want to live out our Father's will as Jesus did. Jesus said, *I did nothing of my own except what the father tell me.* He is our perfect example. If Jesus connected to heaven to download the manual for his existence on earth, we have no other way of living a fulfilled life than to follow in his steps.

You might however say that, Jesus did not marry while he was on earth. It is true that he did not get married to a woman and this is because he already has a bride prepared for him – His Church. So, we have all we need to learn about marriage from the example of Jesus and his bride, the church.

It is true the Word of God says:

"He who finds a wife finds a good thing and obtains favor from the Lord" (Proverbs 18:22)

However, this bible verse has been wrongly interpreted by some in the body of Christ. I have heard it taught many times, that Adam, instead of taking responsibility for his action in the garden, pushed the blame to God and Eve by responding to

God that, it was the woman you gave me who gave me the fruit, and I ate it. There has been claim that because of that response from Adam, God has left man to source for his partner since then. To me, that did not sound like what the God I know and believe in would do. His Word says that He knows the end from the beginning. He knew man would transgress because He created him with power of choice. God's relationship with man from the beginning was never designed as a dictatorship. If His way with man was to be that of "once you mess up, you are finished", I don't think He would have been coming down in the cool of the evening to fellowship with Adam and Eve. There would never have been anything like salvation.

God is holy and His holiness could no longer allow man within close proximity to Him after the sin in the Garden. Still, He did not leave man to himself, He immediately put a temporary plan in place for man to live by, until the salvation plan would unfold, and man can safely, freely, and joyfully approach God directly again. The stop-gap plan was being communicated to man in different manners and at different times as stated below:

"God, who at various times and in various ways spoke in time past to the fathers by the prophets" *(Hebrew 1:1)*

God still guides men on how to choose their partners whenever they are willing to listen. Therefore, God never pushed the responsibility back to man. Now, if He did not, why then does the bible say - *He that finds a wife finds a good thing and obtains favor from God?* I think we have misunderstood what that bible verse is telling us. God's plan for man's existence before the fall and after the resurrection of Christ remains the same, Jesus came to communicate the language of God's grace to us, so to understand that scripture, let us see how Jesus taught us to **"find"**.

Ask, and it will be given to you; seek, and you will find; knock, and it will be opened to you. For everyone who ask, receives, and he who seek, finds, and to him who knocks, it will be opened. Or what man is there among you who, if his son asks for bread, will give him a stone? Or if he asks for a fish, will he give him a serpent? If you then, being evil, knows how to give good gifts to your children, how much more will your Father who is in heaven give good things to those who ask Him! (Mathew 7: 7-11).

This is how Jesus taught us to find - by seeking in prayer.

Mathew Henry's Concise Commentary has this to say regarding the above passage: **"Prayer is the appointed means for obtaining what we need. Pray; pray often; make a business of prayer and be serious and earnest in it. Ask, as a beggar asks alms. Ask, as a traveler asks the way. Seek, as for a thing of value that we have lost; or as the merchantman that seeks goodly pearls. Knock, as he that desires to enter into the house knocks at the door. Sin has shut and barred the door against us; by prayer we knock. Whatever you pray for, according to the promise, shall be given you, if God see it fit for you, and what would you have more? This is made to apply to all that pray aright;**

every one that asketh receiveth, whether Jew or Gentile, young or old, rich or poor, high or low, master or servant, learned or unlearned, all are alike welcome to the throne of grace, if they come in faith. It is explained by a comparison taken from earthly parents, and their readiness to give their children what they ask. Parents are often foolishly found, but God is all-wise; he knows what we need, what we desire, and what is fit for us. Let us never suppose our heavenly Father would bid us pray, and then refuse to hear, or give us what would be hurtful". I have no words to explain it better.

It is He that finds a wife (by seeking counsel from God in prayer), that finds a good thing and obtains favor from God. *Every good and perfect gift is from above, and comes from the father of lights, with whom there is no variation or shadow of turning.* God's favour covers every area of our lives; His favour makes us whole. Thank God that even in the context of; our discussion here, which is marriage, the favor does not just come once, it is continuous (*obtains*) as the need arises. When a man seeks the face of

God in prayer, he is seeking a good thing, his missing rib, which God has upgraded to what his heart longs for, for his completion. A suitable partner (his wife), is not an addition to him but an inclusion. That is why when a man and a woman come together, they do not become two, they simply become one whole flesh. It was the rib that God took out of Adam that He did the "God thing" with, without interference from Adam and He gave her back to him to make him whole again. A good woman would not be a good wife to just any man but the man that she has been created to complete. There must be a mutual fitness (consider how a jigsaw puzzle fits together). Truly, there is no way you can get your perfect match without the help of the manufacturer Himself, so, ask Him! I can tell you for a fact that God cares about you and your choice of marital partner like a father.

I remember sharing a testimony of a lady that have had several visits to heaven with my children. One of her friends or colleagues gave the lady a little note to give to Jesus for him when next she visits heaven. She laughed but collected the letter from the gentleman. So, when she had another visit to heaven and met Jesus, Jesus asked her about the note, and she was with it in her hand. That was amazing!

Later in the day, as I knelt beside my bed to pray, my teenage daughter came to me and said, could you please help me ask God how I would know who my future husband is when it is time? I was like, really? I just laughed and said okay. Then I went back into prayer and said God, you have a message. She wants to know that stuff that she just mentioned. Amidst my shock as a mother who just realized that her 14-year-old daughter is concerned about that 'grown-up' issue, I could not hold back my laughter. Then I heard "send her a note from me and ask her to talk to me herself about it, I am her Father". I quickly tore a piece of paper from my jotter and picked up my pen to write. When I wrote the first letter, the pen faded out and would not write again. So, I pulled out my special pen from the drawer and wrote God's message back to her. As I finished, I heard the silent voice again said, "She doesn't like blue biro". It was then I realized that the first biro that faded out was blue, and the other one I later used was black. You will never catch my daughter using a blue biro! Honestly, if I was asked to mention ten things peculiar to my daughter, that will not come on the list despite the fact that whenever I do shopping for our stationaries, I always buy blue pens for the rest of the family and black for her because she will not write with blue biro, yet God knows and remembers that! He actually paid attention to that. I was humbled. And as months passed, God spoke to her directly on her question.

While a lot of people hear God speak to them through dream, vision, inner witness and many other ways, some people have testified that when they met their God-ordained partner, they knew without a shadow of doubt that this is the right person. The good thing is that divine help is made available whenever we pray. However, God cannot be limited by human expectations. He speaks any way He chooses. It does not matter by which means He speaks; He can speak with or without sound, with symbol or no symbol, in the open or in secret, during the day or in the night, in the time of peace or during time of chaos, when you are awake or when you are asleep. One good and certain thing is that, when He speaks to you, you will hear. It is left for you to either obey or not. One thing we must get right before we begin to ask Him to speak to us is our motives. God said in His Word:

"I the Lord, search the earth, I test the mind, even to give every man according to his way, according to the fruit of his doings" (Jeremiah 17:10)

If your desire is to do the will of God, and not to marry for financial security, social status, sexual satisfaction or any other selfish reasons, but with divine purpose and eternity in mind, then you can be sure God will answer and lead you in the right path to a partner that will complete you. We can fool others and even try to be clever with ourselves, but God can never be deceived.

If you seek His face with a sincere heart, He will not deny you an answer. The answer, remember, may

not come to you as it comes to brother A or sister B. But the answer will surely come. How to choose a husband or wife begins for Christians by deciding to follow God. As a believer in Jesus, you need to build your life on the Rock – which is Christ Jesus, and not on the sinking sands of modern culture and reasoning. ***If you want a rock-solid marriage, you must build your marriage on the Rock***.

DEVIATION FROM DIVINE PATH

When Adam and Eve began their *lovey-dovey* in the Garden of Eden, the bible records that:

"And they were both naked, the man and his wife, and were not ashamed" (Genesis 2:25)

They knew each other completely; there was no lie or deceit. They were completely open with one another, with no need for one to try to impress the other. There was no competition, only pure and unbiased love for one another. They were both one flesh created in the image of God, functioning as intended by God. Flesh without the knowledge of good and evil. Flesh in the purest form.

Then the devil came in to deceive Eve, Adam also fell for the deceit and their **flesh** became corrupted. The contamination did not only create gulf between man and God, it also set Adam and Eve against each other. They ceased to function as one flesh and they began to turn against each other. Disunity that causes competition became evident.

Though the woman was not cursed as the serpent was, she was punished for her complicity; and her punishment was twofold. First, God greatly multiplies *"her sorrow and her conception"* that is, her sorrow generally, especially in connection with pregnancy and childbirth, but also *"your desire shall be to your husband."* In the sin she had been the prime actor, and the man had yielded easily to her persuasion. Henceforward she was to live in subjection to him. God is saying that Eve would desire to rule over her husband, but her husband would instead rule over her. Instead of the mutually interdependent relationship the Lord had created, there is now a desire for one spouse to dominate the other. Sin had wrought discord. The battle for gender equality and superiority was birthed here. Both man and woman would now seek the upper hand in marriage. The man who was to love, care for and nurture his wife, would now seek to rule over her, and the wife would also desire to wrest control from her husband.

It is important to note that this judgment only states what will take place. God says that man and woman will live in conflict and their relationship will become problematic. The statement *"he shall rule over you"* is not a biblical command for men to dominate women. It is a repercussion of the sinful act of disobedience.

In the New Testament, God affirms His ideal relationship between man and woman in marriage. Christ-like qualities are emphasized. What the curse of sin created, believers in Christ are called to correct by living according to God's Spirit. *Ephesians 5 says that the wife should willingly submit to her husband's authority in the home, refusing to scratch the curse-fueled itch to seize control (verses 22-24). Husbands are to love their wives unconditionally and sacrificially, just as Christ loves the Church (verses 25-30).* The whole passage begins with an emphasis on mutual submission to one another: *"Submit to one another out of reverence for Christ" (verse 21).*

From the beginning, God's plan has been for mutual love and respect between a husband and his wife. Though sin has tainted the original beauty of this relationship, God commands believers in Christ to pursue this ideal relationship. When a man goes into marriage with the desire to control and have his wife subjected to him, what he simply desires is to have a marriage that is still established under the curse in the garden of Eden. And the same goes for a woman that desire not to submit to her husband in marriage but who wants to operate from the faulty mentality of gender equality. Man and woman are never equal and will never be! No matter what the modern world or any movement says. The instruction from the bible; to *"submit to one another"* explains it all. The word **submit** means to accept or yield to a superior force or to the authority or will of another person. If they are both equal, then there will not be any need for the word **submit**. The word submit is used because both man and woman have their special place of **authority** in marriage because of what they carry, what has been divinely kept in their custody for the benefit of their partner. They have both received the **authority to yield**, not to withhold, these divine treasures that are meant to be cherished and delivered to one another in fear and reverence for God. Authority is the power and right to act in a certain capacity and is given by someone of a higher power or being. So, in administering such authority, a wise heart should always remember the source and purpose why such authority was given in the first place so as not to be guilty of misappropriation.

Man and woman are uniquely created by God in such a way that one is not lesser than the other, yet they both need each other to be complete. Understanding the beauty, both inward and outward,

of woman (because I am one) makes me marvel at and fall in love with God repeatedly. When both man and woman utterly understand their identity in God, none will either see other as lesser or strive to be like the other. They are individually beautifully and wonderfully crafted. When we approach the marriage institution with this understanding, there will be fewer problematic marriages, because both parties with this understanding will act in God's ordained way and they will be a united force that the devil will never be able overcome. *Note: one force that the devil will never be able to overcome, not attack!*

There may be times when a marriage will face challenges. From the beginning, devil has been at war against the purpose and plan of God. Bible tells us that:

"And from the days of John the Baptist until now the kingdom of heaven suffers violence, and the violent take it by force" (Mathew 11:12)

From the time John the Baptist started announcing the coming of the Messiah and telling people to turn from their wicked ways and its consequences to the saving grace of God, the attack of the devil has increased in intensity. The devil wants to continue to be in control of the world as he has been, but the divine plan of God is for the coming of Jesus to empower as many as will believe in Him to enforce the establishment of God's kingdom here on earth.

In the aspect of marriage, it is the desire of the devil to make all people, including Christians, operate under the cloud of the curse placed on the union between man and woman in the Garden of Eden. You will recall that the man and woman came together and became one flesh. So, the fruit of flesh that enemy, the devil wants to continue to manifest in marriages today are the works of flesh (contaminated version of flesh) listed in the bible verse below:

"Now the works of the flesh are evident,

which are: adultery, fornication, uncleanness, lewdness, idolatry, sorcery, hatred, contentions, jealousies, outbursts of wrath, selfish ambitions, dissensions, heresies, envy, murders, drunkenness, revelries, and the like; of which I tell you beforehand, just as I also told you in time past, that those who practice such things will not inherit the kingdom of God" *(Galatian 5:19-21)*

God said the two shall come together and become one flesh. Did I just hear you say if the works of the flesh are those, then why will God bring man and woman together to become one flesh? Bible recorded that God looked at everything He created, and it was good. God's intention from the beginning was perfect, including when He brought man and woman together and made them one flesh. The flesh was in the image of God and was supposed to continue to reflect the perfect image of God, because God said *"let us create man in our image"*. He created Adam from the dust; Adam was not a whole man after Eve appeared on scene, because God took a rib from Adam to create Eve. He put in her

things that are meant for both of them. Therefore, Adam looked at Eve and said, *"indeed this is bone of my bone and flesh of my flesh."* Genesis 2:23

They complemented each other. They were perfect together and God blessed them. God would not have blessed the works of the flesh that are listed in Galatians 5:19-21, because they are contrary to His nature. However, when man fell in the Garden of Eden through the deceits of Satan, the flesh that was blessed by God got contaminated to the extent that man could no longer recognize his flesh and bone (wife), without the leading of the Spirit. Thank God for His provisions from the foundations of the world. Even before the fall of man, God has in His magnanimous heart, made room for the restoration of the fallen flesh back to the image of God for those who accept the provision.

So, as believers, we know for sure, that we have been redeemed from every curse. When the devil tries to push what was in existence before our redemption back to us, we must shut him up by enforcing what now holds– the Kingdom of God here on earth. There may be times and seasons of challenges; but we are assured that we will always overcome. Do you know why? God said despite the pronouncement of punishment in the Garden of Eden, He is still in control. Before the judgment was pronounced in the Garden of Eden, a provision was already put in place for its removal, for as many as are in Christ Jesus, who walk not after the (**contaminated**) flesh. He says in:

"Behold, I am the LORD, *the God of all flesh. Is there anything too hard for Me?" (Jeremiah 32: 27)*

By the time we bring those works of flesh under the authority of God, they become irrelevant. We ride over them. Every stumbling block become a steppingstone and every blessing, peace, harmony, and comfort that we have lost due to sin in the Garden of Eden has been restored back to us through the blood of Jesus. Howbeit, we cannot cut corners to get it, we must follow the ordained path. Jesus did not promise us a battle free journey with him, in fact, He stated it clearly that:

"These things I have spoken to you, that in me you will have peace, in the world, you will have tribulation but be of good cheer for I have overcome the world" (John 16:33)

Jesus is so sure of his victory of the cross, that as he was praying the last prayer for us before he went to the cross in John 17, He told the Father:

"I do not pray that you should take them from the world, just keep them from the evil one and sanctify them by your truth – Your Word is Truth!

In other words, these ones are ready to rule in victory by the revelation of your Word, the Truth. As mentioned earlier, marriage is the only institution that awards certificate at the point of entry into the institution. This is because the certificate is not a certificate of achievement, but that of enrolment into a walk of victory over curses and judgments for those who are willing to follow the path of the Creator of the institution. Little wonder that Jesus carried out his first miracle at a wedding feast! The bible gave the account of His first miracle like this:

On the third day a wedding took place at Cana in Galilee. Jesus' mother was there, and Jesus and his disciples had also been invited to the wedding.

When the wine was gone, Jesus' mother said to him, "They have no more wine."

"Woman, why do you involve me?" Jesus replied. "My hour has not yet come."

His mother said to the servants, "Do whatever he tells you." Nearby stood six stone water jars, the kind used by the Jews for ceremonial washing, each holding from twenty to thirty gallons. Jesus said to the servants, "Fill the jars with water"; so, they filled them to the brim. Then he told them, "Now draw some out and take it to the master of the banquet." They did so, and the master of the banquet tasted the water that had been turned into wine. He did not realize where it had come from, though the servants who had drawn the water knew. Then he called the bridegroom aside and said, "Everyone brings out the choice wine first and then the cheaper wine after the guests have had too much to drink; but you have

saved the best till now." What Jesus did here in Cana of Galilee was the first of the signs through which he revealed his glory; and his disciples believed in him"
(John 2:1-11)

The institution of marriage is especially important to God because he has designed it in such a way that all other institutions on earth, including the Church, have their roots in the marriage institution. We must also remember that every account written in the scripture have, beyond the letters, a lesson that God wants us to learn through the help of Holy Spirit and apply to our lives.

At that wedding, Jesus and his disciples were invited. Now, that was not the only wedding ceremony that happened during Jesus' lifetime, but we were specifically told that **He was invited** here. The ceremony started as usual and everybody including the bride and the groom were having a good time. They have made their budget in advance, how much food will be required, the quantity of wine that will satisfy their expected guests. Everything was going on as planned until suddenly, they ran out of wine.

Before we continue, have you ever experienced a sudden switch in your well-planned life, program, event, career, or business? Even in marriage, no matter how well you and your partner plan and work hard on how you want your marriage to be, you only have control on your own plan until external parties are involved – both physical and spiritual. It will get to a point that your plan may not be adequate or feasible any longer, because of circumstances beyond your control. It does not mean that you are a bad planner or a poor executioner of your carefully laid out plan; it is just the external world that your human wisdom has no control over. Now, what happens following external interference?

It is such a joy to know that the same special guest at the wedding in Cana in Galilee is still open to invitations into marriages today, even in a better way. He can honour your invitation at the planning stage, so that you would not need to call for damage

control in the middle of the ceremony. Your whole married life should be a life of joy and celebration. This is what God designed it to be, but we must invite Him in from the beginning so we can have it the way He meant it to be for us.

The marriage institution is so paramount in God's agenda for man that the display of Jesus' glory, as recorded, began at a wedding ceremony.

CHAPTER 2

Various labels have been used by sociologists to define the mood or mentality of the world we live in. For example, The Stone Age refers to the era when metals were first used. The Iron Age was a period of economic development, where iron and steel enabled a greater use of metal tools, which were stronger than previous Bronze Age items. The Renaissance was a period in the late Middle Ages, which saw a rebirth of culture, arts, science and learning. The Information Age refers to the era of new modern technologies, which have shaped the modern world. These technologies include computers, the internet and mobile phones.

If an era is defined by what people have most

on their minds and what fills the media, the most accurate description of our current time will be the Sex Age. I cannot remember a time when sex has been more openly flaunted, with so many people obviously obsessed with the subject. It has saturated the society in such a way that anyone that is not in the flow appear as an outcast. In fact, it is as if its abuse is not an issue that deserves attention. How did we get here? What happened to spiritual, moral and cultural uprightness? Gone are the days that you will hear of sexual immorality in the church or fellowship and people that are not even part of the act will weep and pray for the parties concerned. Rural communities in times past use their seasonal festivities to openly expose sex offenders through songs, in order to discourage others from engaging in such activities. This new age seems to have wiped away almost every sense of decency when it comes to sexuality. Anything and everything are overlooked and accepted.

Sexual awareness has always existed as this is natural in the human mind. But today, it is incessantly

stimulated by sex-saturated shows, entertainment, social media, movie, music, comedy and what have you. It is no longer treated with dignity or respect. Many may call it sexual awareness, but in actual fact, it reflects a high degree of ignorance. We are in a kind of sexual wasteland, lacking proper directions and guidance. Sadly, this situation has cost societies dearly in many major ways such as financial losses, health crises, marriage and family breakdowns and a lack of sexual fulfilment and happiness. Very few understand the purpose of sex. It is seen by many as tool of trade, some sort entertainment or affirmation of social status.

The plain and often overlooked answer is that God reveals that He created both sex and marriage. God has a wonderful reason for creating sex. Ignorance of God's purpose for sex has brought about enormous problems. Why then did God create sex? Let us consider the reasons. Not necessarily in order of importance.

PROCREATION

When God finished creating Adam and Eve in the Garden of Eden, the bible records that *"And God blessed them, and God said unto them, Be fruitful, and multiply"*. This statement from God that they should multiply is part of the blessings that He pronounced on them. This multiplication is achievable through sexual intercourse between Adam and Eve, that is, **man and woman within marriage.** An air of sacredness saturates the process described here. God gave a blessing to the creation of children through a loving sexual relationship. God sanctified sexual relations between married men and women, in that the first command He gave Adam and Eve was to begin an intimate sexual relationship and reproduce!

God basically repeats His command, adding another crucial thought:

"Therefore, a man shall leave his father and mother and be joined to his wife, and they shall become one flesh" (Genesis 2:24)

In speaking these words, God formally established the institutions of marriage and family. Since God created and commanded these relationships, marriage and the family are holy institutions, not mere creations of human society.

We see here God's clear intent that children should be conceived and born into a family relationship, a family consisting of a man and a woman, husband and wife.

Historically this has been the norm. But the last several decades have produced a drastic departure from God's pattern. People have tried to redefine the family in all kinds of ways. Make no mistake: God's Word reveals it is a serious error to profane sex and marriage in this way, even as societies are already experiencing the bitter fruits of people trying to do things their own way. God's reasons for creating sex include the purpose of reproduction. But His specific intent is that it should occur within the divine institution of marriage.

SEXUAL PLEASURE

Sexual interest between man and woman is not restricted to the woman's fertility period, either monthly for procreation or over the productive life of the human being. Typically, humans develop a strong interest in sex beginning at least by puberty and may, if they remain healthy, they stay sexually active long after their reproductive years. There are several verses we can reference in the bible, especially in the book of Proverbs and Songs of Solomon, regarding sexual pleasure.

"As a loving hind and a graceful doe, Let her breasts satisfy you at all times; Be exhilarated always with her love" (Proverbs 5:9)

"Your stature is like a palm tree, And your breasts are like its clusters. "I said, 'I will climb the palm tree, I will take hold of its fruit stalks.' Oh, may your breasts be like clusters of the vine, And the fragrance of your breath like apples" (Songs of Solomon 7:7-8)

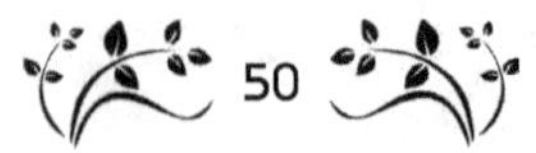

God created a *continuing* sexual interest and sexual appeal in human beings. This, in itself, is a healthy trait of the human mind, which is triggered by hormones that God designed our bodies to produce. Apostle Paul advised married couples that:

"Nevertheless, because of sexual immorality, let each man have his own wife, and let each woman have her own husband. Let the husband render to his wife the affection due her, and likewise also the wife to her husband. The wife does not have authority over her own body, but the husband does. And likewise, the husband does not have authority over his own body, but the wife does. Do not deprive one another except with consent for a time, that you may give yourselves to fasting and prayer; and come together again so that Satan does not tempt you because of your lack of self-control. But I say this as a concession, not as a commandment." (1 Corinthians 7: 2-6)

Sexual drives are strong, but marriage is strong enough to contain them and provide for a balanced and fulfilling sexual life in a world of sexual disorder.

The marriage bed must be a place of mutuality, with the husband seeking to satisfy his wife and the wife seeking to satisfy her husband. Marriage is not a place to "stand up for your rights"; it is rather more like a decision to serve the other, whether in bed or other terms. Abstaining from sex is permissible for a period of time if you both agree to it, and if it is for the purposes of prayer and fasting, but only for such times. Then both parties should come back together again. Satan has an ingenious way of tempting us when we least expect it. This scripture, among many, tells us that God intended for married couples to enjoy sexual pleasure aside procreation.

THE POWER ROOM

Psalm 19 - The Perfect Revelation of the Lord! I cannot explain why; but I am drawn to the beauty and power of this Psalm like no other. I realized that I am not alone in this admiration for this Psalm when I came across this comment on it:

"I take this to be the greatest poem in the

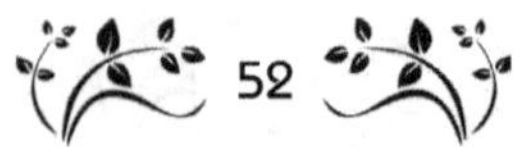

Psalter and one of the greatest lyrics in the world. Most readers will remember its structure: six verses about nature, five about the Law, and four of personal prayer. The actual words supply no logical connection between the first and second movements. In this way, its technique resembles that of the most modern poetry. A modern poet would pass, with similar abruptness, from one theme to another and leave you to find out the connecting link for yourself. But then, he would possibly be doing this quite deliberately. He might have, though he chose to conceal, a perfectly clear and conscious link in his own mind which he could express to you in logical prose, if he wanted to.

I doubt if the ancient poet was like that. I think he felt, effortlessly and without reflecting on it, so close a connection, indeed (for his imagination) such an identity between his first theme and his second, that he passed from one to the other without realizing that he had made any transition. First, he thinks of the sky, how, day after day, the pageantry we see there shows us the splendour of its Creator. Then, he *thinks of the sun, the bridal joyousness of its rising, the unimaginable speed of its daily voyage from east to west. Finally, of its heat: not, of course, the mild heats of our climate, but the cloudless, blinding, tyrannous rays hammering the hills, searching every cranny. The key phrase on which the whole poem depends is "there is nothing hid from the heat thereof." It pierces everywhere with its strong, clean ardour. (Reflections on the Psalms* by C. S. Lewis (New York: Harper One, 1958), pp. 73-74. Van Gemeren).

Looking at this Psalm, it may appear disjointed, but it is not. Though it appears disjointed looking at the actual words, but each part flows perfectly into the other when the Spirit of God takes you beyond the letters; then you get to know the heart of God as He inspired the writer. The first part talks about the message from the heavens and this message is broad, strong and glorious. The heavens, the firmaments, day and night all in unison are communicating the wondrous and majestic works of God to the whole world. The phrase **"Utters speech"** is stronger in the Hebrew text than it appears to be in English, for the

image is literally of a gushing spring that copiously pours forth sweet, refreshing waters of revelation. In these mysterious heavens and firmaments that do not have sound, or should I say the heavens and the firmaments with unsounded voices, God decided to set a tent for the sun. When the sun goes out during the day and performs its duty to the world, it comes back to its tent at night to recharge for the next day. Its source of refueling or recharging is hidden in the tent that God has made for it in the heavens and the firmament.

The heavens declare the glory of God; And the firmament shows His handiwork.

Day unto day **utters speech**, *And night unto night reveals knowledge.*

There is no speech nor language where their voice is not heard.

Their line has gone out through all the earth, And their words to the end of the world. In them He has set a tabernacle for the sun,

Which is like a bridegroom coming out of his

chamber and rejoices like a strong man to run its race.

Its rising is from one end of heaven, and its circuit to the other end; And there is nothing hidden from its heat.

Reading through this Psalm for the first time, you might ask what it has got to do with sexuality. The bible says:

"It is the glory of God to conceal a matter, it the glory of kings is to search out a matter" (Proverbs 25:2)

Bearing in mind that we cannot have access to the mysteries of God, except by His divine grace at work in our lives through His Holy Spirit; we know that when a revelation comes to us, it comes at a time and season chosen by God himself and for a particular purpose. This insight could not have been timelier than now, when every society is experiencing what I call a *sexual epidemic.*

Who can fail to appreciate the beauty of the sun running its course? Who can fail to notice its

steady progression across the sky? Who can fail to recognize its significance? The sun not only lights up our days, it also produces the light and warmth necessary to sustain vegetation, animal life and human life. Without the sun, the earth would merely be a frozen and lifeless rock. When the sun comes up in the morning, it is a glorious sight, much like the sight of a bridegroom emerging joyously from the bridal chamber, with a big smile on his face and swagger to his strides. As the sun works its way across the heavens during the day, it is like a strong man ready for a good run, exulting in his strength and the feel of wind in his face.

This sun that everybody can feel its impacts; its energy, its power and its service as the main source of light to all living things; has its power source mysteriously concealed, hidden away from the knowledge of man, in the heavens and the firmaments by God. This is a mystery; and verse 5 says that *the sun is like a bridegroom coming out of his chamber.* Why did the Psalmists say bridegroom? Why not husband? Why not just a man? It could have been written as *"like a husband coming out of his bedroom or like a man coming out of his matrimonial room?"* But the bible chooses specifically to use the word "Bridegroom". Every word used in the bible is carefully chosen and intentionally used by the writers as inspired by the spirit of God. It is only on the wedding day that man is usually referred to as the bridegroom; from the day after the wedding ceremony and going forward, he is referred to as husband. The coming out of the sun being compared to a bridegroom coming out of the bridal chamber is really amazing! Part of the sun's energy is directly felt or visible to man (the heat and brightness), this is however infinitesimally small when compared to the unseen power (life giving and activating energy) of the sun and its effects on the whole earth. So also, the stride and bright appearance of a bridegroom is nothing, compared to the divine, energy and activating power he has received from the bridal chamber, especially when he is the one that broke the seal as every bridegroom is meant to be honored to do. It is a good thing that the sun does not come out just once in lifetime or once a year, it comes out as often as daily, depending on your geographical location. The husband too has unlimited access to the bridal chamber.

"In them (the heavens) *he has set a tent for the sun"* (verse 4b). God provided a tent for the sun, where it can retire to rest during the night. *"which is as a bridegroom coming out of his room, like a strong man rejoicing to run his course"* (verse 5). If the Lord would compare a bridegroom to this extraordinarily important element in his creation, then He is surely telling us something huge. After the first night, the man and his wife are at liberty to have sexual intercourse with themselves (the marriage chamber) as often as possible and whenever this happens, there is rest and renewal of divine *energy to become* and *power to activate*. I believe *this is the divine creative power that God took out from Adam as a rib* when He caused a deep sleep to fall on him. He shaped this power part (Eve) in such a way that Adam was excited when he saw her. She was shaped and fashioned to complete and satisfy every desire in her man. Have you observed that when a man

wants to boast of his prowess or show off, he beats his chest as if to tell whoever is listening that, yes, 'I did it' or 'I can do it'?. The beating of the chest is a subconscious affirmation of a man's wholeness. God took a rib out of Adam's chest, his place of strength, to create Eve. This means his **can do** strength is incomplete without his missing rib (woman).

Adam was whole before the creation of Eve. When the power part was taken out of him, he became one man, less the power part (I don't know the fraction of one that was), and he remained that way until the first marriage was instituted in the garden of Eden. Every unmarried human male specie is less than one or better put, is not whole or complete until he is joined to the 'rib' that was taken from him at the creation. As stated in the previous chapter, you cannot afford to just pick any power part you come across if you must function well according to the design of the manufacturer. Just like the HP laptop manufacturer will advise their customers to ensure that the battery is recharged with the power pack that is manufactured specifically for the laptop or other gadget manufacturers will also advise their customers to use the charger manufactured for that particular product to avoid malfunctioning of the gadget; so also have we been encouraged to seek the spouse that makes us complete and fit for purpose as designed by God. We cannot afford to pick randomly, even if our would-be choice is born-again. We are individually designed for a particular purpose.

Verses 7 – 10: "The law of the Lord is perfect, converting the soul; The testimony of the Lord is sure, making wise the simple; The statutes of the Lord are right, rejoicing the heart; The commandment of the Lord is pure, enlightening the eyes; The fear of the Lord is clean, enduring forever; The judgments of the Lord are true and righteous altogether. More to be desired; are they than gold, Yea, than much fine gold; Sweeter also than honey and the honeycomb"

Now that we understand that the bridegroom emerges just like the sun does from its mysterious hidden place concealed by God; this implies that the

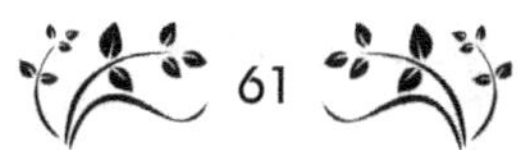

source of energy, the source of power, the source of creative ideas for business and enterprise, the source of fulfilment of purpose, the source of great energy to make things happen, the source of light for illumination, insight and the revealed knowledge is concealed firstly in that bridal chamber on the night that a man first knows his wife (the day that every man getting married is referred to as the bridegroom). This is the breaking off of the seal, giving access to the honey pot for a family; because God has deposited in the bosom of a woman, what her ordained husband needs to combine to his own deposit to rule on earth. It is important to note that a woman does not singularly possess the full required energy (she is a fraction of a whole), otherwise, there will be a bias towards the female gender. Both man and woman possess a percentage of it, and their coming together is what makes the energy whole and adequately productive in the way it has been planned by God. God has deposited a great wealth of it in the bosom of a woman to be treasured, to be cherished, to be protected and only to be released to the bridegroom, for him to function as a man in the full capacity that God has created and ordained him. The same also applies for men, as every man is full of treasures that need activation by his completing power counterpart. The seal been broken by either of the party or both before they come together as husband and wife, is such a costly distortion of divine procedure, but sadly overlooked by many. I still find it exceedingly difficult to understand, when we do or act contrary to the ordained plan of God, expressly disobeying His commands and expect no repercussion for our actions. We do not create ourselves, we have a laid down principle we must follow from the Word of God regarding every aspect of our lives, yet because time is always changing, with new man-made ideas constantly evolving, we expect the one who created time and seasons to change with what He has created. No, *in Him there is no variableness nor shadow of turning.* His commands were not given out of circumstances or situations. Man is created to fit into God's ways and ordinances, not the other way round. In the above Psalm, the psalmist clearly stated the importance of paying attention to the laws, testimonies, statutes, commandments, fear and judgement of God. It is not by chance that these were specifically mentioned in this portion of the bible, where God chose to reveal the mysterious power of a bridegroom as compared to emergence of the sun. I wholeheartedly believe that if we keep His commands relating to marriage and relationship between a man and his wife, 90% of the problems in the world today will not even exist to begin with. A healthy marriage means a healthy family, which in turn produces a healthy society. The writer of this Psalm, King David, ended the rendition with a personal deep prayer, because he has tasted the bitter outcome of sexual immorality. This is a good lesson from an experienced victim.

There is so much importance attached to sexual intercourse that we cannot afford to continue in our ignorance and expect things to turn around for good. There are two stories in the bible that I will like us to look into for more understanding regarding sexual intercourse and its power. The two stories happened in the household of King David. The first one is the account of Absalom, when he plotted to

overthrow his father, King David. The King fled with his trusted men; and for Absalom to further affirm that he has taken over the power and authority of rulership from his father, the bible records this:

"So, they set up a tent on the palace roof where everyone could see it, and Absalom went in and had sex with his father's concubines" (2 Samuel 16:22).

And by so doing, Absalom laid further claim to the kingdom; and, as it were, took possession of it.

Secondly, when Solomon became king after the death of King David, Adonijah (David's eldest surviving son, who declared himself king if not for the timely intervention of King David who commanded the enthronement of Solomon), persuaded Bathsheba, king Solomon's mother, to entreat the king to permit him to marry Abishag. Abishag was the beautiful young girl that was chosen to care for and lie with the aging King David when he was old. She was chosen for the task with great care on account of her virginity, youth, beauty, and physical vigor, to serve the king as a practical nurse. That Abishag was

married to David before she laid with him, and was his secondary wife, appears from its being imputed as a great crime to Adonijah that he desired to marry her after his father's death. Although David had not "known" Abishag, that is, had no sexual relations with her, nevertheless she was considered *an inheritor*, and with her could go the *rights to the throne*. Having once failed in an attempt to seize the kingdom, Adonijah now sought in a more subtle way to achieve his objective. Solomon suspected this request as an aspiration to the throne, since Abishag was considered David's concubine, and so ordered Adonijah's assassination (1 Kings 2:17–25).

In the earlier story of Absalom's rebellion, it is noted that having sex with a former king's concubine is a way of proclaiming oneself to be the new king. The same goes for Adonijah.

Just as it was in biblical days, this belief and custom is still in play in the tribe I come from in Nigeria, which is the Yoruba land. It might be the same with other tribes in Nigeria or in Africa at large, but I can only speak of the one I am very certain of. It is a taboo for another man to sleep with a king's wife, whether she is still married to the ruling king or not. If such happens, both the woman and the man should be executed under customary laws (now superseded by modern laws). Also, a king is not permitted to have a concubine; he is rather expected to marry any woman that he has sexual intercourse with. Customarily, such acts outside marriage causes death for an erring king. The way modern age has affected many aspects of human existence, the office of kings I believe is no exception. A lot of laid down rules and moral culture have been overlooked and discarded without regards. Back in the days, the word of the king comes with power and is revered, but in the recent past, a lot of our kings have been subjected to insults and ridicules by many people without any repercussion. Have you ever wondered why? It was said that when a king has a concubine, that is, sleeping with a woman that is not married to him (and the woman eventually moves on in life and gets married to another man), customary folklore and an old saying claims that such will result in the

death of such a king. I'm sure when it happens the first time and the king remain alive; life goes on and iniquity persists. Little did they know that the death that was implied is not a physical death; it is the death of purpose! There were words that God allowed to be uttered through the mouth of men that they themselves do not know the magnitude of what they have declared. The power to rule no longer resides with some of our kings because of sexual immorality. The power and authority to rule is not a license to do as a king pleases; it is rather a mandate to rule in the fear of God.

"The God of Israel said, The Rock of Israel spoke to me: 'He who rules over men must be just, Ruling in the fear of God". (2 Samuel 23: 3)

Any misappropriation of sexual desire, appetite and power is a death sentence for divine purpose. One Sunday afternoon in April 2019, I was in my room and like in a flash I just saw a garden of flower with low yet secured fence around it. Then I saw a man holding water hose entered the garden; he turned

on the tap to water the garden. Then strangely, he stretched his hand over the fence, pointed the water hose outside the garden and instead of watering the flower plants in the garden, he was just pouring the water outside the fenced garden, wasting it. When the scene cleared, I asked God what that meant. The Lord said to me when couples are making love and one of them is thinking about someone else, that is, fantasizing about another person instead of concentrating their passion and all the feelings that comes with it on their spouse, they have simply behaved like that man in my vision. They have wasted a source of nourishment and energy meant for that marriage and if this continues over time, the fence around the garden is at the risk of collapsing.

A lot of people that have been in sexual relationship(s) before they get married or even while they are married may suffer this attack from memories of those unholy relationships. God has called us into a life of fulfilment and perfection, but if we refuse to work with Him from the beginning, then we cannot blame him when we face the challenges

and the outcome of our disobedience. The word of God says: *"If the foundations be destroyed what can the righteous do?" Psalm 11:3*

CHAPTER 3

This chapter is especially dedicated to every youth in Nigeria, who in one way or the other has been affected by the current state of the nation economically, socially, religiously, and politically. An average Nigeria youth is creative, intelligent self-motivating and a fighter. However, the wealth and power seams to reside with another generation, the older one. The big question is why?

The **Lazy Nigerian Youths** (hash tagged "**#LazyNigerianYouths**"), is a social media revolt by Nigerian youths against certain comments made their President, Muhammadu Buhari. While speaking at the Commonwealth Business Forum in Westminster on Wednesday, 18 April 2018, President Buhari said, in response to an interviewer's question about a totally unrelated topic, that a lot of Nigerian youth have not been to school and want everything free (including education and healthcare), because the country is an oil producing state. Young Nigerians thereafter took to social media to protest this comment.

As the youth protested, I felt their pain and I understood what they were saying. I could see a lot of youth these days that are much younger than my own generation, struggling with the limited resources they have at their disposal to become an entrepreneurs, developing and evolving under a very harsh economic condition.

When I consider the way youths in Nigeria think, and their struggles to make ends meet, I marvel and wonder where they get their ideas and energy from. Looking back at when I was growing up, all that my generation knew and wanted to do was to go to school, get good grades and get a white-collar job. My own generation would rather find solace in a white-collar job, just enough to make their families comfortable. Not that there was anything wrong in that; but the present creativity level of our youth has exposed the previous generation's laid-back way of thinking. We were highly active with our brains, but our creative minds were rather passive. We were too comfortable with what our parents' thought were good for us, without looking inward to really discover who we were created to be.

An average youth today will ask you three questions for every instruction you give; not out of rebellion, but rather to feed their inquisitive minds. They are the generation that does not like to beat about the bush. They love to have the end picture in mind before starting. More than ever before, a lot of the youth in university today already own a business alongside their studies and 70% of these businesses are duly registered companies. Those that are not privileged to go to school are equally pulling their weight in the society, business wise. I am privileged to work a lot among youths in my church, and this has given me the opportunity to see how engaged

economically most of them are. But I must say, the energy they put into these businesses are not in any way commensurate with the returns they are getting from the businesses.

With all the struggles going on in their lives and no matching returns, hearing such a statement from their own President could be heart wrenching and devastating. They sure did react the best way they could. I reacted in a different way, not because I wanted to, but because Holy Spirit just kept bringing it back to my heart day after day until I realized this is God and He must be calling my attention to something, then I started thinking about this particular controversial statement from Mr. President in the place of prayer and study of the Word. The first place God directed me to in the bible was John 11:51, where Caiaphas unconsciously prophesied that Jesus should die for the whole nation. Here is the commentary on the verse:

And this spake he not of himself: but being high priest that year, he prophesied that Jesus should die for that nation;"

And this spake he not of himself. — There is a moral beauty in the Word, in spite of the diabolical intent with which they are uttered; and Apostle John adds the explanation **that they had an origin higher than him who spake them.** Writing after the events, he has seen them fulfilled, and regarded them as an unconscious prophecy. Like Balaam, Caiaphas was an oracle or God in spite of himself, and there were in his words, a meaning far beyond any what he had intended.

Being high priest that year, he prophesied that Jesus would die for the nation — He stood, therefore, in the position which made him the official representative of God to the people, and gave him an official capacity to convey God's truth. This was represented in the days of Samuel by the Urim and Thummim; and John, himself a Jew, still thinks of the high priest's breast as bearing the oracle, which declares the will of God, regardless of any unworthy human thoughts that may have filled the heart beneath. It may be that another reference to the high priest's office is present in these thrice-written words. It was the high priest's duty to: *"enter within the veil"* and *"make an atonement for the children of Israel for all their sins once a year"* (Leviticus 16). **In that year the veil was rent, and the first step taken by which the holy place was destroyed, and the high priest's office ceased to exist.** With the destruction of the holy place, the Jewish day of Atonement lost its significance, **but the high priest that year, by his counsel and action in the Sanhedrin, was causing the sacrifice which should be presented by another high priest, in the Holy of Holies as an Atonement for the world**.

"Christ being come as high priest of good things to come, by a greater and more perfect tabernacle, not made with hands, that is to say, not of this building; neither by the blood of goats and calves, but by His own blood He entered in once into the holy place, having obtained eternal redemption" (Hebrews 9:11-12)

Even though the discussion on ground at the commonwealth forum then was totally unrelated

to President Buhari's response, he still went ahead according to the ordained plan and divine timing to utter the statement about the Nigerian youth. God decided to use him as the head over the nation and a seasonal oracle to get the statement out just like he used Caiaphas in the passage above by virtue of his office as a priest.

What we must bear in mind is that there may be a lot of people that share the same view with the President, but the statement needed to come from Him as the authority and God's allowed leader over Nigeria at that particular time. Also, it is noteworthy that after Caiaphas statement regarding Jesus (who the religious leaders of that time saw as one that did not fit into their expected religious plan and structure), was a divine fulfilment of a long-time prophecy. This prophecy fulfilment surely happened with a lot of shakings and realignments, but the outcome is the birth of the body of Christ, the arrival of the Spirit of God and the hope for eternal life.

As it was then, so it is now. The statement by

the president was not a mistake; it was uttered under a divine prompting and timing. So, while people continued to get angry about it, I started rejoicing because I know beyond every shadow of doubt that *"the people living in darkness have seen a great light; and those living in the land of the shadow of death a light has dawned"* (Mathew 4:16)

When that statement was uttered, there was a shift in the spiritual realm and a season of change was conceived. Just like in the time of Jesus, there will be a lot of shakings and realignments, but all glory to God, there will also be a birth of a new nation, an outpouring of the Spirit of God and fulfilment of purposes.

The truth, no matter how odd it sounds, eventually sets free. The bible says *you shall know the truth and the truth shall set you free (John 8:32).* When we hear something or we think we know something, most of the time, our human minds process only the letters and arrive at a conclusion that is usually far from the truth. Let me illustrate what I mean with this example:

Imagine a woman that realizes that her husband is cheating on her. A lot of thoughts will start running through her mind amidst her pain and confusion like: what have I done wrong, am I not attractive enough, is it that I'm not good in bed, did he marry me for some ulterior motives and many more. After a lot of unanswered questions, she finally decides to go on her knees to pray, and in the place of prayer, the Holy Spirit opens her heart to understand that she is not the problem, but that her husband is under a demonic attack that is bent on derailing him from the path of righteousness before he arrives at his place of destiny by planting a strange woman in his life to weaken him spiritually and eventually destroy him. Now the **truth** has been revealed to her, beyond the level of what her logical mind or voices from friends and advisers can fetch her. Her victory or otherwise then depends on her reaction or response to the revealed truth. She can decide to team up with the revealer of the truth and fight on her knees or if foolish, she can decide to finish the battle in the physical which I am certain she cannot win.

I have said all that to say: President Mohammad Buhari, as ordained by heaven, made that statement to reveal the truth that will set as many youths that are willing to embrace the truth free. The statement has been reacted to by different people at different level, even up to senate level. But were the reactions based on the truth or the letters?

THE INIQUITY OF THE LAND

As creativity is in high wave among the youth, so also is a certain vice that has driven many to the hands of destiny destroyers. It is the vice of materialism. I have never seen a generation that is as *designer label crazy* as this present generation. It is natural with humans, that anything that is withheld from us is excessively chased or longed after. Due to the level of poverty in the land, materialism has become an idol being worshiped. Even basic things in life have become luxury that many people are unable to afford. When the devil wants to turn a man to a murderer, he will not come straight to him and start waving a flag of murderer at him. The enemy's strategy is always subtle, and it usually slips in quietly and unnoticed. Regarding the youth, suddenly, everybody wants to appear grown up, flaunting expensive designer bags, shoes, clothing, cars amongst others. Is there anything bad in using all these things? Emphatically no! If you can afford them without crossing into sin, please go ahead and enjoy them. But, must you chase after these material things? No! However, for this present generation, in order to satisfy the excessive craving for materialism, they are willing to trade anything, especially their bodies in sexual pleasure to older males and sometimes females (who keep on getting rich at their expense), just to get money to satisfy their lust for materialism. This vice of materialism is the devil's subtle and clever way of stealing the future of the youth, through which he deflects and rebrands them from what God has created them to be. Their attention is quietly shifted away from desires to preserve their values, build themselves up to become sources of blessing, impactful people and living out the respective purpose of God for their lives. They just want to have it all and have it now! The aim of the devil is to waste this generation by making them ineffective during their prime years. He is not preventing them from dreaming and having great ideas, but he is draining them of the creative energy to execute such ideas and turn them into reality. A man that is full of ideas but have no peace of mind and resources to execute the idea is worse than a man without any idea.

It is true that we have been taught in churches and from cultures of the land, that it is a sin for a girl to be deflowered and for a man to engage in sexual intercourse before getting married, this has always been noted to be a sin against God. Yes, sure it is. An errant youth thinks that, since our God is merciful; when we confess our sins and turn away from them, he forgives us, right? Oh yes, our God surely does. However, there are two things I want you to have at the back of your mind regarding sexual sin:

1.　*Flee sexual immorality. Every sin that a man does is outside the body, but he who*

commits sexual immorality, sins against his own body. Or do you not know that your body is the temple of the Holy Spirit who is in you, whom you have from God, and you are not your own? For you were bought at a price; therefore, glorify God in your body and in your spirit, which are God's (1Corinthians 6:18-20).

This clearly shows us that, when you indulge in sexual immorality, your own body suffers the consequences. Now, I am not talking about wear and tear of our physical body. Remember the above passage also says that *our body is a temple of God.* There are sacred and holy contents, divine treasures, and Presence, kept and available inside the temple for the spiritual benefits and fulfilment of every one of us. What happens when your temple is desecrated? You hurt yourself badly! Something major is taken away from you! The structure of the temple might remain intact, but the Spirit of God is far from such temple. The divine Presence that makes ordinary to become extraordinary is no longer in defiled temples. An access way is also given to nature to determine what happens in such temple, since the Spirit that enforces the supernatural is no longer there.

In fact, we see how this is related to losing a divinely inputted right and placement in the bible:

"Lest there be any fornicator or profane person like Esau, who for one morsel of food sold his birth right" (Hebrew 12:16)

Why was Esau referred to here as a fornicator or profane? To be profane means to have no care for divine things, but only for the gains and pleasures of this world. It means to cast away a spiritual privilege for immediate gratification.

"And Jacob gave Esau bread and stew of

lentils; then he ate and drank, arose, and went his way. Thus Esau despised his birth right" (Genesis 25:34).

Esau both ate and drank and rose and went away; This is a very graphic example of a profane mind. Little did Esau realize that his path of destiny has been reconstructed, due to his immoral act of not holding dear what has been committed into his hands for his lineage.

2. If you suffer a major wound on your body and you go to the hospital, the wound would be dressed and treated, after some time, it would heal up, and you would not experience any pain again. The truth is that, even when there is no longer any physical pain, there would be a scar that will always remind you of the wound incident.

Sexual sin, no matter how modern age

trivializes it and make it look as if it is okay to sleep with whoever you want, anytime, anywhere, without any regard for the Word of God, the consequence is much more than you can imagine. Each time you engage in immoral sexual activity, you are losing great grounds to the enemy. Your treasure chest, the honey pot, is opened for the enemy to loot at will. What is taken away will work wherever it is taken to, knowingly or unknowingly, because it is a life-giving energy. At times, it even gives life to negative things that adversely affect society. There was a day I came across someone's whatsApp status that read "After you first night with him, on your way home you see his status update, 'DONE AND DUSTED', what will you do? ME: I will update mine, Mission accomplished, another destiny wasted, glory taken, then switch off my phone". That definitely says a lot about what is going on in the world. For someone to casually put that up on social media where millions of people can see it means it is not something new to this generation yet many still engage in casual sex like people without control.

The enemy has attacked this generation with the strategy that was used in the Garden of Eden. The devil did not go for Adam; he went for Eve. So also, today, the enemy is targeting our young girls first to deal his blow on this generation, by planting desires in their heart for what they cannot afford to buy themselves, while they are still young. They have fallen for the deceit of men in the older generation, who give them money and material things in exchange for their divine treasures for creativity.

When a girl is deflowered by any other person apart from her husband, it is a huge loss that may never be recovered, except by the special mercy of God. It is an unimaginable loss! Even as a born-again Christian, you will make heaven because you have repented from your sin, but you may never live a perfectly fulfilled life if it is not specially addressed.

A lot of young girls have sold their virginity to older men, who have money to buy them material things. They do not know that by giving themselves away to these men, they are giving away God's deposit of wealth and success, the creative energy deposited in them, that is meant solely for their God-ordained husbands when they get married; the older generation sees them as cheap commodities, to be bought, used and discarded when a newer and better one appears. By the time they eventually get married later in life, they are almost empty of the energy they are empowered with by God to combine with their husbands' during sexual intercourse, for him to prosper with and give them a satisfying life. Their husbands may be hardworking, but the power that gives life to labor and turns it to success has been wasted by their wives long before they get married. Virginity is no longer a virtue in today's marriages; and this is really sad.

As God was giving me revelations for this book, I kept asking in my spirit, will everybody not think I am going crazy? Considering the way sex and all related atrocities has consumed the society and has become a norm. You will hear of people having sexual intercourse with several partners concurrently and insisting it is not wrong. Teenage girls now willingly offer themselves in pairs to men for sex, in exchange for money; and they feel no remorse or any sense of loss. Young men also do likewise, often casually; they would sleep with older women for money, without realizing that they go in full and come out empty, inadvertently mortgaging their destinies for a few t-shirts, a pair of jeans and a pair of boots. Later, when they realized that things are not going the way it should for them, they settle for the evil money ritual option. They sacrifice their female peers by having sex with them in order to get what the herbalists require from them for the money ritual. The youth are unconsciously fighting a spiritual and sexual war with one another, leaking away the creative energies meant for their generation.

I believe God saw the confused state of my heart and sent one of my mentees to me. She called me one morning and said, "so those things you have been telling us about sex are true." I asked her how she knew they were true. She then narrated a dream she had the night preceding her call. According to her, in the dream, she was warned not to sleep with any man before she gets married, because the source of her husband's breakthrough for wealth will be through their first sexual intercourse encounter. She was further informed in the dream, that one man that knows how to cunningly use evil divination to seek information about people's destiny will later come her way, pretending to love her, but it is only to steal from her. The liar will only approach her because of the unique treasure chest deposited in her bosom, and he will do everything humanly possible to sleep with her. If she makes the mistake of allowing him to have his way, he will later dump her because he would have gotten what he wanted and when she eventually gets married, her family will live a life of struggles. In her dream, she was given specific details concerning the strange man; including how they will meet.

While she was thanking me for encouraging her

to stay away from sexual immorality; I was thanking God for confirming everything he has asked me to put down in this book.

Think about it, society will change, many things will evolve, morals will lose its value, but the Word of God stands sure from generation to generation. His principles and ordinances never change.

There is such a great mystery surrounding sexual intercourse that a lot are not aware of; hence, they use it as a tool of trade to meet their immediate needs in exchange for their legacy. Little do they know that they are selling their future and the wealth mapped out for their generation to another. It is not a sin that brings repercussions on just one person or the duo that partakes in it, it robs everyone in their lineage of their glorious destinies and the impacts may not even end with a generation. In other words, sexual immorality could have a ripple effect on many generations. What a tragedy!

You may ask why the devil is focused on young females majorly? The truth is that nothing

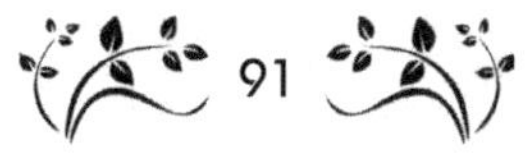

just happens. There is a spiritual background to everything we see in the physical. This generation did not plan their world to be like this, neither is it the will of God for them. Though every man will bear the consequences of his sin, but the preceding generations has bitten sour grapes and the teeth of the children are now set on edge. The festival of Art and Culture held in Nigeria in 1977 (**FESTAC '77**), was the sour grapes that Nigerian leaders ate, for which the teeth of the younger generation are now set on edge. The mask for the festival was the miniature representation of Queen Idia (a **female goddess**, mother of a king who ruled in 16th century in the old Benin Kingdom). Her face was uplifted as god by our nation in 1977.

We should all recognize and note the significance and importance of symbols. Symbols are expressions of thoughts, in form of images, which are set with the intention of making it stay on or to be strongly impressed upon the hearts of men, both consciously and unconsciously until it becomes permanent. The FESTAC '77 mask was the image of a god that we lifted up for the invited countries, as the provider of our wealth and affluence; we invited other countries to come and join us in celebration. We were even generous enough to allow them bring their own idols and gods too. After all, the more the merrier, right? What the organizers failed to realize is that, whatever you lift above God in your life, loses God's protection. We have lifted up a female goddess, Queen Idia, as our god; we have told the almighty God of heaven to move aside, that our female is powerful to be in charge. Little wonder the most travelled people earlier in Nigeria were from Benin State (now Delta state and Edo state). Then, all roads led to Italy; and we all know what happened to our precious daughters that embarked on these perilous trips. The repercussions started right at the origin of the raised deity, Benin!

Nigeria has been a country rich in mineral resources, well before the discovery of petroleum oil. The oil was an additional source of blessing to Nigeria. The oil boom of the 1970s brought about the emergence of disorderliness in Nigeria. It brought about a total shift from peace and blessings to chaos and curse. Nigeria's then President, General Yakubu Gowon, boasted that the problem of Nigeria is not money, but how to spend the money. Words are powerful generally, but they are more powerful when they emanate from the mouth of anyone in a position of authority. It could have sounded like an ordinary boastful statement, but it attracted the attention of every demon of greed, waste, and corruption; and Nigeria's problems began after this.

Although General Olusegun Obasanjo and others claimed, and are still claiming that FESTAC '77 was the celebration of black Arts and Culture; where was the place of God in the festival? A festival where 50 countries came together with their different idols; and openly celebrated idolatry with the wealth given to the land by the God of heaven and earth, the Almighty? The festival was a pure worship of demons and idols! What really happened was, that our leaders took our God given resources and threw parties for demons. The devilish festival went on for 29 days! (January 15 – February 12, 1977). When

the festival ended, the invitees physically went back to their countries; but the demons they came with built their embassies in Nigeria and never left!

Whether you believe it or not, there is a demonic covenant entered into during this festival, which is not known to the rest of us; but the people that entered into it and sold the nation to demons are well aware of what they did. If openly, during the festival, they could be reciting incantations, you should imagine what would have happened behind the scene; hidden away from sight of innocent citizens.

The older generation has perpetrated this evil; and now the innocent generation is paying dearly for it. The painful part is that they have stolen and still stealing from this generation, mainly through forbidden sexual intercourse; with the so called *sugar daddies and aristo* sleeping with the young girls, with or without charms, and giving them peanuts in exchange for the divine power that is meant for them to empower their own husband to

build a home and secure an economically balanced future for their offspring. What a wicked generation! A high percentage of our young ladies have very little or no regard for their femininity. They would rather fall for the devious manipulations of the older men, acquire material wealth for themselves, get underserved and accelerated placements or promotions at the work place, and become so independent that no man within their generation would be good or bold enough to earn their respect or admiration as a suitor. Then the men in turn feel so little and start engaging in different types of dubious ways, from internet fraud to money making rituals, just to earn respect by hook or crook. The young males too no longer have respect for the females in their generation because they know how the ladies would rather prefer the wicked older men to them. So, there is resentment from both sides, to the extent that when they eventually get married, it is just to fulfil family or societal expectations. In some instances, the forbidden sexual relationship continues after they get married. How do we expect the blessings of God on such unions?

This is just like the story of King Ahab and Naboth in the bible (1 Kings 21). A vineyard is a plantation of grape-bearing vines, grown mainly for winemaking, but also raisins, table grapes and non-alcoholic grape juice. A vine is of a lasting value, which is usually passed from one generation to another. On the other hand, vegetables are meant for immediate consumption – the need and desire of a profane mind as we will all recall. King Ahab here, who has lost his influence and power as a king to his demon possessed, blood thirsty and idol worshipper wife, Jezebel, now had so much time at his disposal to be shopping for a vegetable garden. What a twisted king! And of all the land available in the land then, it was Naboth's vineyard that appealed to his greedy appetite. What do you expect from a senior profane citizen, who has lost his ground to the idol worshipper he invited into his life and palace, that eventually unseat him from his throne of influence, rulership, authority and power? He wanted to remain relevant by any means, even if by converting a legacy (vineyard) into an ephemeral circus tent (vegetable garden).

This is akin to the situation our youth have subjected themselves to. The young girls have bitten the bait of the "Sugar Daddies" or "Aristo" as the perverted male adults are often referred to in my country – Nigeria; they continue to open up their honey pot and hand over the source of the creative energies of their generation to wicked adult men, thereby rendering their own generation lazy. The older generations use their ill-gotten wealth to throw big parties and invite young men that should be in positions of power, making business and political decisions, to come and crack jokes for them. Abomination! A huge percentage of young people in Nigeria are now comedians. The sad part is that most of them are brilliant professionals, who turned comedians just to make ends meet. The power has been stolen! Young ladies, young men, you have both betrayed one another. A house that is divided against itself cannot stand. It is time to go back to the beginning - God, so you can reach your expected end.

In any society, where wealth distribution is not

balanced, you will notice in the background of such community, a sexually imbalanced relationship of the older generation having forbidden relations with the younger generation. This is generational stealing. We are all busy complaining that the politicians and the people in authority are stealing the nation's money to enrich their pockets; but no! That is not totally correct. It is not only the money they are stealing; but also, the creative energy from our young vulnerable ladies, the creative energy deposited in them for their future partners in marriage. **Wherever the energy resides, that is where the money flows.** The younger ones are unknowingly empowering the older ones to steal from them and are at the same time rendering themselves lazy youths, who are void of power to create or executive creative ideas. So sad!

We have a remarkably interesting conversation between Laban and Jacob recorded in the bible passage below:

"After Rachel gave birth to Joseph, Jacob said to Laban, "Send me on my way so I can go back to

my own homeland. Give me my wives and children, for whom I have served you, and I will be on my way. You know how much work I've done for you."

But Laban said to him, "If I have found favour in your eyes, please stay. I have learned by divination that the Lord has blessed me because of you." He added, "Name your wages, and I will pay them" (Genesis 30:25-30)

Let me refresh our memory on Jacob's journey to his uncle, Laban's house. When Esau sold his birth right to Jacob for a plate of porridge, I am sure he would have thought in his mind, "let's see how you collect the birth right, you fool". He forgot there was a mutual agreement and exchange. At the right time for the birthright to be activated, events and nature teamed up with Jacob to activate the switch of rights. On getting to know that the careless barter he made with Jacob was not a joke, Esau was ready to take back what he thought was his by all means. Rebecca, their mother, and the brain behind the switch of the birth right, advised Jacob to run to her

brother, Laban's house for safety.

Jacob therefore carried away the blessing of his father's house, the birthright of the firstborn, to another man's house. It did not matter that the birthright was not with the original owner, it was still continually active, because it is an unseen energy force that does not die, irrespective of location and the custodian. Laban was harvesting the blessing meant for Esau without any apology. It was another exchange – "I put roof over your head Jacob, you submit the blessing you carry to me". Esau's birth right blessed the house of Laban while Jacob was busy slaving away under his uncle. Jacob only survived on whatever Laban gave him. He was thoroughly cheated and used. When he came to his senses and demanded for his freedom, his uncle did not mince word to tell him that he knew he was getting rich at the expense of Jacob's.

Let us come back home now. All the wealth that has been stolen and is still being stolen by our elders, what exactly is happening to it? They steal from their children, their own land, and people; just

like Jacob did to Esau, they carry the stolen wealth abroad, where their own children ran to and slave away as second-class citizens. The land where these blessing are carted away to are getting richer and better, while our children dwelling in the land are being cheated and paid peanuts for their hard labor, in the land where their stolen treasures are hidden. Is it not time for us to wake up and cry out to God for restoration? Yes, it is. We must turn back from our wicked ways and seek God that He might forgive and heal our land.

CHAPTER 4

One thing that I have observed in the bible, and that I still cannot fathom its depth, is the way God makes ready provisions for our salvation from sins and its consequences. I am not talking about being born-again alone, but also of God rescuing us from destructions when we blindly and eagerly turn away from the path of righteousness. Each time we fall and run back to Him, He is ever ready to accept and restore us. Another amazing part is His mercy that actually draws us unto repentance, not because we are tired of or too grown up to commit sin. How would a mortal man know how to turn away from wickedness and seek holiness, if not by the prompting of the Spirit of God. In the old testaments, there are many instances that the people will commit sin, God will raise a prophet to tell them how they have turned away from Him, the penalty for their sins and that they should turn back to Him so he can save them. When they eventually do, you will be amazed the way He will turn against any city or kingdom that has dealt wickedly with his people and punish them severely. He will then bless his people and it will be as if they never strayed. But first, they must heed his call and turn back from their sinful way.

All through the new testament also, since the time of John the Baptist, people have been preached to, to turn away from their wicked ways, accept the Lord Jesus Christ and receive a new life. Even after you accept Christ, if you find yourself back on the path of destruction, there is a provision for redemption that is already made available for us in Christ:

"My little children, these things I write to you, so that you may not sin. And if anyone sins, we have an Advocate with the Father, Jesus Christ the righteous. And He Himself is the propitiation for our sins, and

not for ours only but also for the whole world" (1 John 2: 1-2)

Next, we are told how we should affirm our confession of knowing Jesus:

"Now by this we know that we know Him, if we keep His commandments" (1 John 2:3).

If we claim to know Him; we must do as He commands. We cannot say because we are in the dispensation of grace and the effect of sin after the resurrection of Jesus is not as it was in the old testament; we can continue to live a double life. We cannot continue in sin and ask for the grace to abound. The wages of sin remain death:

"For the wages of sin is death; but the gift of God is eternal life through Jesus Christ our Lord" (Romans 3:26).

REPENTANCE

God is beckoning to this generation and I strongly believe He is starting with Nigerian youth. There has been a strong wave of the Spirit of God among the youth, which has given birth to a lot of true worshippers; and I believe that this is to prepare the heart of this generation for the new move of God, soften their hearts to receive the Word of God in spirit and in truth and step out of playing religion. I pray that these worshippers will endure, and that they will not burnout before their salvation is perfected. They will see the birth of their new nation in Jesus name.

God is calling on the youth to turn away specifically from sexual sin. Did I hear you say that will be a tall order? No, it will not. When God is ready to move, nothing can stop Him. He created men and He rule in their affairs.

Now is the day of God's power to visit this generation and turn their heart back to Him. He said in His word that in the day of His power, His people shall be willing, Psalm 110:3. I love its exposition as shown below:

"Thy people shall be willing in the day of thy power, in the beauties of holiness from the womb

of the morning: thou hast the dew of thy youth.
In consequence of the sending forth of the rod of
strength, namely, the power of the gospel, out of
Zion, converts will come forward in great numbers
to enlist under the banner of the Priest King. Given to
him of old, they are his people, and when his power
is revealed, these hasten with cheerfulness to own
his sway, appearing at the gospel call as it were
spontaneously, even as the dew comes forth in the
morning. This metaphor is further enlarged upon, for
as the dew has a sparkling beauty, so these willing
armies of converts (from spirit of lies and religion)
have a holy excellence and charm about them; and
as the dew is the lively emblem of freshness, so are
these converts full of vivacity and youthful vigor, and
the church is refreshed by them and made to flourish
exceedingly. Let but the gospel be preached with
divine unction, and the chosen of the Lord respond to
it like troops in the day of the mustering of armies; they
come arrayed by grace in shining uniforms of holiness,
and for number, freshness, beauty, and purity, they
are as the dewdrops which come mysteriously from
the tooming's womb. Some refer this passage to the

resurrection, but even if it be so, the work of grace in regeneration is equally well described by it, for it is a spiritual resurrection. Even as the holy dead rise gladly into the lovely image of their Lord, so do quickened souls put on the glorious righteousness of Christ and stand forth to behold their Lord and serve him. How truly beautiful is holiness! God himself admires it. How wonderful also is the eternal youth of the mystical body of Christ! As the dew is new every morning, so is there a constant succession of converts to give to the church perpetual juvenility. Her young men have a dew from the Lord upon them and arouse in her armies an undying enthusiasm for him whose "locks are bushy and black as a raven" with unfailing youth. Since Jesus ever lives, so shall his church ever flourish. As his strength never failed, so shall the vigor of his true people be renewed day by day." (Bible Study Tool).

Just the way God would require the Israelites to clean up by washing themselves when He is about to visit them, He is asking us to do the same now by cleaning ourselves from every form of sexual

immorality. However, our cleansing this time is not that of outward part, but of our hearts.

So, how do we begin our cleansing? The first step is to ask God for forgiveness of your sin. God says in His word that:

"if My people who are called by My name will humble themselves, and pray and seek My face, and turn from their wicked ways, then I will hear from heaven, and will forgive their sin and heal their land." 2 Chronicle 7:4.

We have God's assurance that when we confess our sins and turn away from them to follow Jesus, He will accept us and never turn us away. Then we must humbly complete our cycle of obtaining full forgiveness by receiving and activating the power that Jesus gave us after his resurrection.

FORGIVENESS

After resurrection, when Jesus appeared to the disciples at the upper room, listen to what happens:

"Then, the same day at evening, being the first day of the week, when the doors were shut where the disciples were assembled, for fear of the Jews, Jesus came and stood in the midst, and said to them, "Peace be with you." When He had said this, He showed them His hands and His side. Then the disciples were glad when they saw the Lord. "So Jesus said to them again, "Peace to you! As the Father has sent Me, I also send you." And when He had said this, He breathed on them, and said to them, "Receive the Holy Spirit. If you forgive the sins of any, they are forgiven them; if you retain the sins of any, they are retained" (John 19:20-23)

Please pay attention to verses 22 and 23. When Jesus breathed on them, He said *"Receive the Holy Spirit"*. That is what they needed to prepare them for the task ahead of them. It is amazing how the preparation was to start, which the next verse explains. It is to forgive! Wow! These were the people set aside to birth the Church of Christ; to proclaim the maiden edition of the Gospel of Truth. For them to be fit for the purpose of their calling,

they must begin at the place of forgiveness. He did not ask them to proceed to mountains to fast, pray or start preparing speeches. He did not ask them to develop strategies on church planting or growth. He breath upon them and said receive the Holy Spirit. If you forgive the sin of any, they are forgiven them, if you retain the sins, of any, they are retained. The first thing that Jesus' resurrection power brings to humanity is the power to forgive sins; because that is the message of the cross where new life begins. Remember that the problems we have discussed in previous chapters started because there is deviation from the plan. Another life has been offered to us now and the place to begin living the new life is the place of forgiveness. Without that power to forgive, the disciples would never have been ready for the baptism of the Holy Spirit with evidence of speaking in new tongues. The bible records that Jesus appeared to them several times during the forty days He spent on earth after His resurrection and all he was telling them after that first visit was about the kingdom of God. During His last visit, He told them not to leave Jerusalem until they receive

what the father has promised, and He told Peter to feed His sheep. However, when He breathed on them and gave them the initial gift of Holy Ghost, it was for power to forgive. The foundation for the new season!

For the move of God for this generation to fully start, we must forgive our leaders! Including our parents, uncles, aunties, or anyone that has been in a place of authority over us, that we believe has offended us.

No matter how you have felt the weight of that national sin of FESTAC'77, no matter what your grievances are towards your leaders in the family, communities or religious bodies; they are weights that CANNOT go with us unto the next level. They must be dropped. The danger of not letting go and forgiving is that if we hold on to them, according to the bible, they stay with us together with their effects. The effects of the errors of our leaders are the injustice, corruption, blood shedding, that we are facing today. We do not want them again;

therefore, we must forgive, so that God can remove all the negative effects. Jesus did the same before he fulfilled purpose. He asked the Father to forgive those who crucified him, before He fulfilled his purpose of coming to the world. His death was His purpose, His resurrection is our victory. He died for us; we will live for him.

God will not demand from us what he has not deposited in us. Thank God for Peter's question to Jesus -

"Then Peter came to Him and said, "Lord, how often shall my brother sin against me, and I forgive him? Up to seven times?" Jesus said to him, "I do not say to you, up to seven times, but up to seventy times seven". (Mathew 18:21-22)

No matter how annoying you think someone is, it will be almost impossible for such person to offend you 490 times in one day; but here is Jesus responding to Peter that you should forgive one person that much. Are you really going to start marking every offence on a wall or recording them

in a journal to know when the person has exhausted the 490 counts so you can strike back and have your own pound of flesh? Of course not! What Jesus is simply telling us here is that our capacity to forgive should exceed anybody's capacity to offend us. We are created in God's image and likeness, and He has forgiven our numerous sins; and once we have experienced God's forgiveness and grace in our own lives, we should extend the same to others. No, they may not deserve it — but neither did we deserve forgiveness when God forgave us. It is the kingdom's principle that we must live by, we cannot cut corners. The Bible says:

"Be kind and compassionate to one another, forgiving each other, just as in Christ God forgave you" (Ephesians 4:32).

Our nation is poor, the whole world is extremely poorer than we can ever imagine! Every single person on earth is created in the image and likeness of God. I have heard that severally, you say. Let me explain further. There was a dream the Lord showed me

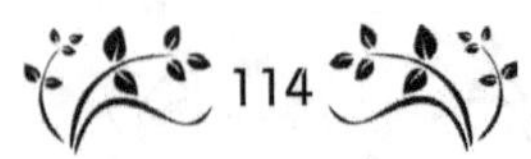

about two years ago. In the dream, I saw a very tall and massive ridge (like Egyptian pyramid except that there was no sharp edge like that of the pyramid. It was smooth and round). There was a simple looking young man that was taking soil from the big ridge and making pots. When he finishes making one, he will place it by the side of the ridge in such a way that the pot is resting with its side on the ridge. The bottoms of the pots were made in such a way that they cannot stand straight on their own but must rest on the ridge. When he finished making the pots, he brought out a bigger pot and started pouring its content into the smaller pots he has made. Two things caught my attention. The first one was that as he takes soil from the ridge to make the pots, the ridge did not decrease. Also, as he pours the content from the bigger pot into the newly made one, the content keeps coming out and never finishes. As I stood wondering, someone appeared beside me and said, that is the Potter Boy. As he said that, I just knew he was referring to Jesus. Then he went further to explain that the content He is pouring into the pots are the portion of him deposited in

each person, which represents the assignment they are to carry out on earth. Their purpose for coming to the world, their destinies. Then I said "oh, just like what God told me I must do for Him here on earth? (Here I was referring to another encounter I had years before this dream, where God told me what I must do for him - my purpose); and he said yes. With that I started moving from one person to another, telling them they have the portion of Jesus in them that they must live out while they are here on earth. I was so excited doing this, that I woke up with a big smile on my face. And the first thing I said was *"Potter Boy"* and busted out laughing. Jesus, the Potter boy, So cool. Naughty me! The feeling I had when I woke up from this dream what that type you have, when you visit a dear friend in her home town, and you heard her been called by her native name for the first time. You know the type of smile that will be on your face! And the feeling that I know him more now, rather than just being a mere acquittance. However, I soon realized that nothing that is revealed about Jesus is new. Everything and everyone were made by Him.

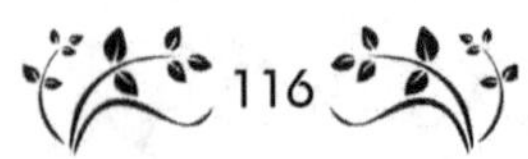

"For by Him all things were created that are in heaven and that are on earth, visible and invisible, whether thrones or dominions or principalities or powers. All things were created through Him and for Him". (Colossians 1:16).

"All things were made through Him, and without Him nothing was made that was made". (John 1:3)

I have met several people, and I know beyond reasonable doubt that they are simply living out the portion of Jesus that was deposited into them here on earth. These people, ranging from gospel ministers, to musicians, artists, health workers, teachers, police; and others; do what they do with contagious joy and ease, that will make others wonder how they are so much at peace doing what they do, while others are apparently struggling to do the same thing. The simple answer is that they have discovered their own purpose. Imagine what will happen if we all live out what our creator has deposited in us from the beginning. What a joy, beauty, harmony, and peace that will be. This is the place that God is inviting these generation into; He

is ready to work with us if we return and submit to Him.

Are we not tired of laboring without reward? He said,

"Come to Me, all you who labor and are heavy laden, and I will give you rest." (Mathew 11:28)

The new spiritual move is coming and as many as are willing will find their place in it. We must turn back from our sexually perverted ways and run back to God. A lot of us are so confused about our identities because we have tapped sexual creative forces from people whose destinies are quite divergent from ours. A young graduate that is destined to be a medical doctor or lawyer, who have slept with different girls that are meant to be married to musicians, businessmen, farmers and engineers, might revel in his sexual prowess on the girls and when done, he is now ready to focus on his future. Little does he know that his focus has been diluted by all the different sources of creative energy he has tapped from. Such a man's focus would have been

severely impaired. Such a young man will suddenly think his destiny is to be an entrepreneur today, two years after that, he would want to become a musician, then after another six months, an entirely different career path would appeal to him. Why? He did not wait to drink from and to stick to his own well as instructed by the word of God. King David in the bible had Abigail, a woman of good wisdom and loyal heart befitting for a king. However, his uncontrolled appetite pushed him to sleep with and eventually married Bathsheba. Bathsheba was a woman meant for Uriah, a warrior. When King David tasted water from her well, he tasted from a well meant for a warrior and he became a murderer. Uriah's well (Bathsheba) was for his empowerment, but to David, it was a strange anointing that turned him to a murderer against his loyal staff. A well that is no meant for you, no matter how sweet it tastes, poisons your spirit.

Solomon, the wisest man in history: he understood the way of the smallest creature to the biggest one. Dignitaries from far and near travel down

to Jerusalem to listen and learn from his wisdom. By the time Solomon finished his adventure of drinking from different well, his conclusion to everything is "Vanity upon Vanity". That was confusion in bold and capital letter!

"Drink water from your own cistern, And running water from your own well. Should your fountains be dispersed abroad, Streams of water in the streets? Let them be only your own, And not for strangers with you. Let your fountain be blessed, And rejoice with the wife of your youth. As a loving deer and a graceful doe, Let her breasts satisfy you at all times; And always be enraptured with her love." (Proverbs 5:15-19).

The same goes for the ladies that have emptied their honey pots to strangers before getting married; such would later complain that their husbands are not able to meet their needs. Most ladies are forced to leave the training of their children to nannies and maids, to seek for means of keeping the family together. There is no substitute that can ever be

equal to motherly care! The excessive long hours that mothers have to spend away from their children during their formative years is telling negatively on our societies today. Let us turn back to God that He may show us His mercy and restore our land.

To man, some things might look impossible; but with God, nothing shall be impossible. The story of the birth of Jesus through virgin Mary and the prophecy against the Samaria famine in 2 Kings 7, among others, confirms this. No matter how terrible your situation seems, you can be assured that if you are willing, God is ready to work with you.

It is time to consciously turn back from our wicked ways. Sexual immorality is a mission to destroy one's destiny. Apostle Paul says:

"Flee sexual immorality. Every sin that a man does is outside the body, but he who commits sexual immorality sins against his own body" *(1Corithians 6:18)*

Run away like you are escaping from something that might harm you because it will ruin you. Even if trending culture despises you for keeping holy, it is better to escape from sexual sin than to be conquered by it. Recall the story of Joseph and Potiphar's wife (Genesis 39:7–12).

Paul shows that sexual immorality is different from other kinds of sin because it is a form of self-harm. We might commit other sins with our bodies, but sexual immorality unites us sinfully with another person. This happens on a deeply physical and spiritual level. We will experience the natural consequences of that sin at that deep level, as well.

As mentioned in the introduction part, no matter where you find yourself in the page of this book, it is not written to condemn you rather it is meant to let you know there is problem so you can run to God who can help you. Do not be like the foolish virgins who went about looking for how to get light when Light himself was coming to them.

"Then the kingdom of heaven shall be likened to ten virgins who took their lamps and went out to meet the bridegroom. Now five of them were wise,

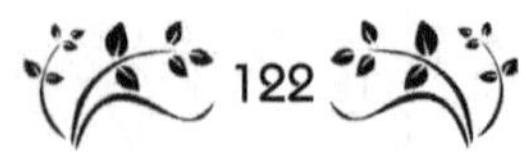

and five were foolish. Those who were foolish took their lamps and took no oil with them, but the wise took oil in their vessels with their lamps. But while the bridegroom was delayed, they all slumbered and slept.

"And at midnight a cry was heard: 'Behold, the bridegroom is coming; go out to meet him!' Then all those virgins arose and trimmed their lamps. And the foolish said to the wise, 'Give us some of your oil, for our lamps are going out.' But the wise answered, saying, 'No, lest there should not be enough for us and you; but go rather to those who sell, and buy for yourselves.' And while they went to buy, the bridegroom came, and those who were ready went in with him to the wedding; and the door was shut.

"Afterward the other virgins came also, saying, 'Lord, Lord, open to us!' But he answered and said, 'Assuredly, I say to you, I do not know you.'

"Watch therefore, for you know neither the day nor the hour in which the Son of Man is coming (Mathew 25: 1-13)

The command that was given to all the virgins was to "go out and meet him". If they were not trying to impress the bridegroom that was coming by quickly getting oil and put on their lamp as if it was never out, they would have simply cry out to him that sir, we have messed up, our lamp is out, please forgive us and allow us to walk in your light. The bridegroom that is coming is definitely not coming in darkness.

"All that the Father gives Me will come to Me, and the one who comes to Me I will by no means cast out" (John 6:37)

Instead of doing that, they went out during the midnight to start looking for oil. Who sells oil by midnight? So, do not think you have gone too far from God or you need to do some work of cleaning up yourself before you cry out to God. He is not looking for people that appears presentable or are emotionally stable, He want us to come to Him as we are.

"Humble yourselves [with an attitude of repentance and insignificance] in the presence of the Lord, and He will exalt you [He will lift you up, He will give you purpose]" (James 4:10 Amplified).

Let us lift our voices and cry out to God for mercy on behalf of our land. Some of us were young and many were not yet born during FESTAC '77; but we must all repent of it before God. You do not get drowned because you fall inside a river; you drown because you stay submerged in it. It is time for us to get out of the water of affliction. No, we will not drown in Jesus name! Remember, just because we choose to forgive our leaders and confess the sin of the land does not mean that individuals who refuse to turn to God personally will not answer to God; but that is not our bit to worry about. Some of the key perpetrators are dead, some are unwilling to turn to Christ because of how far they have gone into darkness; but we all have common denominator — Nigeria. Let us do the needful.

WARNING!

"For the LORD of hosts hath purposed, and who shall disannul it? and his hand is stretched out, and who shall turn it back?" Isaiah 14:27

God's hand to visit the youth in Africa is stretched out and I strongly believe He is starting with the youth in Nigeria. He is ready to visit His land by empowering the youth of the land, turning them from Lazy youth to His own mighty army that will enforce divine plan and purpose according to heaven's agenda. He wants to empower them in the marketplace, on political platforms and corridors of power. This will direct the flow of wealth to their hands, but they must be aligned first. God does mighty miracles but at the same time, He does not break His own kingdom's principle. They must repent from sexual perversion, the source where the energy to be wealthy leaked out from.

The baffling part is that when God is set out to move, he will set out the human vessels He will work through. If they refuse to yield, He will change the

vessels but His purpose and plan will never change.

"My covenant I will not break, nor alter the word that has gone out of My lips." Psalm 89:34

Christian youths, please hear the word of the Lord and be aligned to His purpose. Flee sexual immorality and be equipped, ready for His move. If you do not, He will still carry out purpose. Nigeria will never be pushed back into financial slavery. However, if the Christian youths are not ready, do not be surprised when you suddenly hear of emergence of a secular group that will push "no-sex-before-marriage" movement. It will shame Christian how committed the unbelievers will be so faithful to this cause and grow so powerfully because wealth will answer to them. They will grow and be powerful. They will oversee power and will be the one to dictate to the church. God's wealth principle is no respecter of person or group, anyone that respect the principle will receive the reward. How the reward will be used is what will show whether the receiver is for God or not. God has done this before in the bible and can do it again.

"Thus says the Lord to His anointed, To Cyrus, whose right hand I have held-To subdue nations before him And loose the armor of kings, To open before him the double doors, So that the gates will not be shut: "I will go before you And make the crooked places straight; I will break in pieces the gates of bronze And cut the bars of iron." Isaiah 45:1-2.

Cyrus is a king mentioned more than 30 times in the Bible and is identified as Cyrus the Great (also Cyrus II or Cyrus the Elder) who reigned over Persia between 539—530 BC. **This pagan king** is important in Jewish history because it was under his rule that Jews were first allowed to return to Israel after 70 years of captivity. King Cyrus actively assisted the Jews in rebuilding the temple in Jerusalem under Zerubbabel and Joshua the high priest.

The earth is the Lord and everyone who dwells in it, He will use anyone that is available. He is not after able vessels but available vessels. He is the One that give ability to available vessels to make them able. Be jealous for your place in God's plan. Do away with sexual immorality.

REPAIR

"When I was receiving instruction from the Lord to write this book, I remember asking the Lord that, with the problems of multiple sex partners that this generation has been exposed to, what will God do to sort and restore the lost glories and destinies? I asked this question because so many sexual perversions that cannot be uttered have become widely prevalent now than at any other time. This generation will beat Sodom hands down in sexual sin. I was truly scared for how far we have deviated from the path of decency and fear of God. You know what God told me? He said, "I am still the God of dry bones". Immediately, I flipped my bible to Ezekiel 37: 1-14 that says:

The hand of the Lord came upon me and brought me out in the Spirit of the Lord and set me down in the midst of the valley; and it was full of bones.

Then He caused me to pass by them all around, and behold, there were very many in the open valley; and indeed, they were very dry. And He said to me, "Son of man, can these bones live?"

So, I answered, "O Lord God, You know."

Again, He said to me, "Prophesy to these bones, and say to them, 'O dry bones, hear the word of the Lord! Thus, says the Lord God to these bones: "Surely, I will cause breath to enter into you, and you shall live. I will put sinews on you and bring flesh upon you, cover you with skin and put breath in you; and you shall live. Then you shall know that I am the Lord."'"

*So, I prophesied as I was commanded; and as I prophesied, there was a noise, and suddenly a rattling; and the bones came together, **bone to bone**. Indeed, as I looked, the sinews and the flesh came upon them, and the skin covered them over; but there was no breath in them. Also He said to me, "Prophesy to the breath, prophesy, son of man, and say to the breath, 'Thus says the Lord God: "Come from the four winds, O breath, and breathe on these*

slain, that they may live." ' " So I prophesied as He commanded me, and breath came into them, and they lived, and stood upon their feet, an exceedingly great army.

Then He said to me, "Son of man, these bones are the whole house of Israel. They indeed say, 'Our bones are dry, our hope is lost, and we ourselves are cut off!' Therefore prophesy and say to them, 'Thus says the Lord God: "Behold, O My people, I will open your graves and cause you to come up from your graves, and bring you into the land of Israel. Then you shall know that I am the Lord, when I have opened your graves, O My people, and brought you up from your graves. I will put My Spirit in you, and you shall live, and I will place you in your own land. Then you shall know that I, the Lord, have spoken it and performed it," says the Lord.'"

Lord, let this revival to begin!

The bones are truly scattered as young men and women are so consumed with satisfying their crave for comfort without seeking God's guidance. Could

it be that God's guidance is part of the old school items that does not fit in into the specification of the items we have chosen to bring into the present age. We would rather bury that in the past and engage modern ways of seeking comfort by any means possible: "use what you have to get what you want" as the popular saying goes. God's providence is not limited in any way to a certain time or age. It is alive and relevant to all time and situations. Glory to God for His mercy and assurance of revival.

We may think that after all, we are still alive and how does this scripture apply to the subject we are discussing? Let us look at two scripture that will help us understand how.

While Jesus was here on earth, he offered prayers and pleadings, with a loud cry and tears, to the one who could rescue him from death. And God heard his prayers because of his deep reverence for God" Hebrews 5:7

We all know that Jesus was crucified, and He died on the cross; He was in the tomb for three

days before he resurrected. So, why did the above scripture say *He cried out to the one who could deliver him from death, and he was heard?* Or, what type of death is the scripture talking about here? For us to have good understanding of that scripture, we will need to check the bible passage that recorded where Jesus cried out in prayer to God. Let us check out the second scripture:

"He walked away; about a stone's throw, and knelt down and prayed, "Father, if you are willing, please take this cup of suffering away from me. Yet I want your will to be done, not mine." Then an angel from heaven appeared and strengthened him. He prayed more fervently, and he was in such agony of spirit that his sweat fell to the ground like great drops of blood (Luke 22:41-44)

This is the account of when Jesus prayed fervently to the one who could rescue him from death; but note that the bible was not talking about physical death. If it were to be physical death, Jesus would have escaped the cross, but he did not. He was crucified and died physically on the cross. The death that the scripture is talking about in Hebrews 5:7 is **death of purpose.** The reason why Jesus came to the world is to die for you and me, so he might reconcile us to the father; that was the cup He wished the father could remove from Him – the death he wished Father could deliver him from but He eventually had to submit to God's will to fulfill His purpose on earth. God heard him when he cried out and said, "yet I want your will to be done, not mine".

Though many may be physically alive, but in terms of their destinies, they are dry bones because their purpose of coming to the world is dead. Without the mercy of God, many will just exit the world without living. Almost all are dead purpose-wise due to wrong marriage partners and sexual promiscuity. Some might have even been victims of rape or sex rituals; but whichever category you find yourself, the God that brought scattered dry bones back to life is extending His invitation of restoration to you today. Do not harden your heart.

Our God is not into a patched-up restoration business; He rebuilds from the foundation! He does

not declare His move for a new season because he wants to impress humanity. He does so because that is the next item on His divine agenda for man, and He wants as many of us that are willing to benefit from this move.

"Let the house be rebuilt, the place where they offered sacrifices; and let the foundations of it be firmly laid, its height sixty cubits and its width sixty cubits, with three rows of heavy stones and one row of new timber. Let the expenses be paid from the king's treasury. Also let the gold and silver articles of the house of God, which Nebuchadnezzar took from the temple which is in Jerusalem and brought to Babylon, be restored and taken back to the temple which is in Jerusalem, each to its place; and deposit them in the house of God" (Ezra 6 :3)

If you can repent and allow God to carry out the necessary repair works, your life will surely take a new turn. I cannot assure you that the transition will be smooth because there will be a shaking, a melting down, a remolding and so on but be assured that you will not be alone. Jesus will be with you all the way to the new life in him. You can count on him. This is your season for restoration in Jesus mighty name. Amen!